PUTT PERFECT

PUTT PERFECT

Edward Craig

hamlyn

First published in Great Britain in 2005 by Hamlyn,
a division of Octopus Publishing Group Ltd
2–4 Heron Quays, London E14 4JP

Distributed in the United States and Canada by
Sterling Publishing Co., Inc.
387 Park Avenue South, New York, NY 10016-8810

ISBN 0 600 61269 4
EAN 9780600612698

A CIP catalogue record for this book is available from the British Library.

Printed and bound in China

10 9 8 7 6 5 4 3 2 1

The text has been written from the point of view of teaching a right-handed
player. Reverse the advice given for left-handed players to read 'left' for
'right' and vice-versa.

Photography shot at The London Golf Club

CONTENTS

INTRODUCTION

Putting is the most important element in golf. Perfecting your technique, approach and ability on the green will reduce your handicap more rapidly than any amount of ball-beating on the range. A good ball striker can be a poor golfer because of putting. A good putter is almost always a good golfer.

If you can guarantee to two-putt 90 per cent of the time, then you will be shooting low numbers. If you are two-putting regularly, you'll sink your fair share of long putts, birdie putts, par-saving putts – and you'll be difficult to beat. Even if you spray the ball from the tee, miss the bulk of greens with your approach shots and become inconsistent when chipping, you can salvage a score through simple consistent putting. A weak round can be rescued and a good round can become great.

Putting also remains the most elusive of all disciplines in golf. There are basic rules that you should stick to with your full swing – a decent grip, good posture, good rhythm, and so on. With putting, in reality, anything goes. A solid, basic technique and rhythm is extremely helpful but, to putt well, you need to find an inner touch: a magical, artistic side to your game. Putting is the dark art to the full swing's science. This book aims to help you discover – or rediscover – the personal side to your game. We do cover fundamentals but also reveal secrets – from key thoughts to practice drills, from green-reading skills to psychological tips.

Although putting makes the simple difference between most high- and low-handicap golfers, few amateurs spend time practising, thinking and working with the short stick. This is madness. Which club is used on almost every hole? Which club do you use for half your shots? How often do you use your driver in comparison to your putter?

Putting practice is not fun – in fact it can be quite dull. Ripping (or trying to rip) a driver for 100 balls is more satisfying than knocking 100 putts. This is the second aim of this book – to give you enough ideas to head to the practice greens ready to have fun. Practice-putting is enjoyable if approached in the right way – and it will make your rounds infinitely more satisfying as you break through those 90, 80, and even 70 barriers.

We are presenting here a guide to better putting. Through simple illustrations and step-by-step instruction, you'll discover success on the greens, which leads to success on the course. This is your first step to becoming unbeatable – just don't let your opponents read it.

EQUIPMENT

Before you can putt, you need a putter, but which one? The choice on offer in even the smallest pro-shops or stores is bewildering. Watch any professional event and you'll see that each golfer uses a different short stick. As putting is an uncomplicated technique, you might think putters were simple clubs. This is not the case and using the right putter for you will make a vast difference to your game.

What putters are out there?

You name it, it has probably been invented. There are some huge-headed putters – frying pans on stalks; others, by contrast, have tiny heads, so that hitting the ball is more like striking a marble with a pin. A popular putter from 2002 onwards was a larger-headed model with two circles stuck on the back mimicking the ball.

Putters can have markings on the face, on the top of the club, on the shaft, on the grip – anywhere that might make a difference and help you align yourself more accurately.

The old-fashioned weapons are beautifully crafted blades of metal, simple and elegant in design, without the complications of extra metal and paint. Many putters have extended shafts and grips and some players occasionally feel more comfortable with a shortened stick.

The three main types of putters

Putters can be clearly distinguished by their balance: the way the clubhead rests on the ground. Here is a quick guide to them:

The heel-toe or blade putter

In the early days of golf, there was only one type of putter – a blade. This is the simple, old-fashioned stick that ruled the roost before more inventive manufacturers found a market to exploit with more sophisticated models. It is, in all probability, one of the more difficult types of putter to use for the bulk of golfers, but if you like it and it works for you then stick with it.

Manufacturers have designed putters in all manner of shapes and sizes to help you on the greens.

The rules of golf

A putter is a club with a loft not exceeding 10 degrees, designed for use on the putting green. The shaft or neck or socket of a putter may be fixed at any point in the head. A putter grip may have a non-circular cross-section, provided the cross-section has no concavity, is symmetrical and remains generally similar throughout the length of the grip. A putter can be any length.

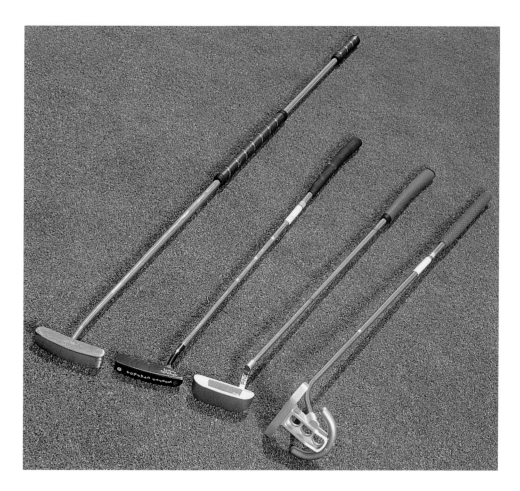

The face-balanced putter

Then along came the face-balanced putter. This is a modern weapon that tends to have more metal behind it, offering a sturdy and steady feel when rested behind the ball. These clubs are more prevalent than blades nowadays and can be easier to strike consistently.

The in-between putter

This is a club that is half face-balanced and half blade. It has the best properties of each, combining the elegant look and feel of the blade with the steady look and touch of the face-balanced putter. It is the design that launched manufacturer Ping as a serious concern in the market.

Remember that there is no putter that will suit everyone. Find one that works for you and that feels comfortable. Spend time on the practice green trying out different types.

Different types of putter suit different players and techniques; there is no overall correct club.

Jargon buster

'Putterface' The side of the club used to strike the ball.

'Putterhead' The whole head of the club incorporating the putterface.

The right putter for you

Choosing the right stick is essentially a matter of comfort. If it feels good and works, don't worry about what you look like – just get on with it. But, when you are next assessing your equipment, decide whether you are using that putter because you like it or because it is the only one you have. It may be time for a change and there are some guidelines that can lead you to the putter that works best for you.

Don't get muddled by the variety of putters available. Ask a professional about the different properties and qualities of each type of putter. Manufacturers often add gimmicks and stylize putters without changing their fundamental properties. Be careful to choose a putter for the right reasons – feel, comfort, fit – and not be wowed into buying an unsuitable stick by clever marketing.

Make your putter fit you

Your putter should fit you; you shouldn't have to fit your putter. So many golfers play with ill-fitting equipment and this leads to funny techniques as they compensate for overly short or extra-long shafts. Don't fall into this trap but find a putter that is the right length for your height. Ideally, when you address the ball, your arms should hang naturally from your shoulders so your elbows are relaxed but naturally straight, not rigid. If your putter is too short, you will have to bend your knees or elbows to make the putter fit your body, causing instability in your stroke. If your putter is too long, you will have to extend your arms to let the putterhead rest behind the ball, and this stretch will see you lose all touch and feel in the stroke. Your arms must hang naturally from your shoulders with the club gently resting behind the ball in your normal address position.

A short putter will make you crouch over the ball.

A long putter will have you reaching over the ball.

A suitable putter will make you comfortable at address.

Make your putter fit your stroke

The different makes of putter can be commonly broken down into three categories. Each category is more suited to one type of stroke than another. Work out which stroke you favour, then try a suitable putter.

The face-balanced putter

A face-balanced putter works best for the players who have a straight-back, straight-through, pendulum stroke – the most common technique. The face of the putter stays square to the target line throughout the stroke – take it back straight, swing through straight and the ball will roll straight. Modern players who use it include Retief Goosen and Colin Montgomerie.

The in-between putter

The in-between putter suits both styles, which is why it is so popular. If you hold all the clubs by their throats and parallel to the ground, the blade hangs vertically downwards, the face-balanced putter stays horizontal to the ground and the in-between putter stays at 45 degrees – it has the best of both worlds.

The heel-toe or blade putter

This type of club suits golfers whose stroke has a swinging-door motion, swung from inside the line to square path (see page 31). Ben Crenshaw was the most famous putter with this type of stroke. His putterhead swung inside the line, then square at impact, then inside again.

A change is as good as a rest

You may find it best to play with two or three putters and keep rotating them regularly, although you can only use one putter per round. Changing your putter can sharpen your stroke and touch – a surprising way to stay in form on the greens.

Three types of putter

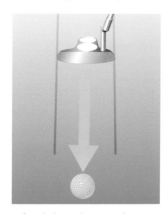

A face-balanced putter suits a pendulum stroke.

An in-between putter suits most strokes.

A heel-toe putter suits a hingeing door strike.

The belly and the broomhandle

There are other types of putter commonly used on golf courses across the world. Their distinct looks raise eyebrows and it is a source of great debate as to whether they are unfair and should be made illegal, yet interest in them is at an all-time high – they are the belly and broomhandle putters. The aim of any putter stroke is to make the ball run smoothly end-over-end. Belly putters and broomhandles when used properly make it easier to get the ball to roll smoothly.

What is a belly putter?

The belly putter is any normal head with an extended shaft and grip. This extended shaft rests in your midriff and you grip down the club in the normal position, with an orthodox hold. The club is not as long as the broomhandle but longer than a regular putter.

What is its purpose?

These putters take your wrists out of the stroke. The butt end of the club resting in your belly gives you a centre-point, making it easy to take a good set-up position. This centre-point or fulcrum holds the club in place as you rock your shoulders through the stroke.

How common is it?

Many of the world's best golfers have used the belly putter – Colin Montgomerie and Vijay Singh being two notable recruits. After great success, Vijay's form dipped and he reverted to a normal-length putter – three months later he was world number one.

The belly putter uses your midriff as an anchor point – or pivot point – so the club is held steady at one end.

Buyer beware

If you are thinking of investing in either a belly or broomhandle, make sure you pick a club that fits. Just because it is called a belly putter does not mean it is a belly for you – take into consideration your height and build and, most importantly, whether the putter is the right size for nestling comfortably in your belly when you are bending over a putt.

What is a broomhandle putter?

This is an altogether longer putter. The shaft is extended further than a belly putter and there are often two grips added, one on the end of the shaft and one in the middle. Techniques to use this club vary but always involve a split-hand grip. Again, the head of the club is identical to heads on ordinary putters.

What is its purpose?

The broomhandle putter became popular thanks to professional golfers' misery on the greens. Professionals can, from time to time, suffer from the 'yips', a distressing problem arising over short putts (see page 44). Out of desperation to cure the yips, the broomhandle was born. The idea is that the hands are taken out of the stroke completely so that the momentum of the club or your shoulders alone moves the putterhead – hands solely hold it in place with zero pressure. The unique grip also uses different muscles from an orthodox hold – this change seems to help keep the club steady.

How common is it?

Many senior golfers use broomhandle putters as the yips often strike as you grow older. Scotland's Sam Torrance and Germany's Bernhard Langer are two famous users of the longest stick and former Masters champion Ian Woosnam flits between this and the orthodox length. It is not as common a sight in the amateur game.

The broomhandle putter looks to take your wrists out of the putting stroke by splitting your hands.

The shame of the broomhandle

There is a stigma attached to the broomhandle putter – an admission of on-the-green failure. The pros admit that you can never be as good with a broomhandle as you are with the short club – conversely, you can never be as bad. It has extended numerous careers.

Jargon buster

'Hold' Another word for the grip – how your hands take 'hold' of the putter.

The grip

Your hold on the golf club is the single most important element in a successful putting stroke. Your grip determines your technique, your feel and your comfort. A good, reliable grip will make the putter solid in your hands and boost your confidence. But, as with every element of the sport, developing good technique requires work and practice. Here is a simple step-by-step reminder on how to build an orthodox – or reverse overlap – putting grip.

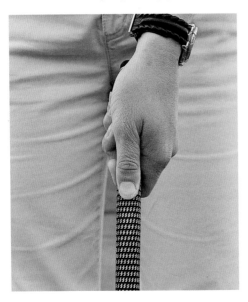

1 Place your left hand on the club, just as you would for a normal, Vardon grip (the most common grip used for a full swing). Let the grip of the club run through the palm of your hand, as opposed to the base of your fingers, as it should for a full swing. Lift the index finger free from the club and, otherwise, keep your grip as similar to your normal hold as possible.

2 Now place the right hand on the club. The key here is to let your right hand fit underneath the left index finger that is not touching the grip. Again, try to run the grip through the palms, as opposed to the base of your fingers. Rest the left index finger on the back of your fingers on your right hand – the opposite to the Vardon grip where the little finger of the right hand sits on top of the little finger on the left. Finally, move your hands together to take a good, comfortable hold of the club. As the grip runs through the palms, it will feel difficult to use your wrists in the stroke – and that is key to producing a good roll.

Too much wrist

A poor grip could lead to too much wrist in the stroke. A wristy technique was used years ago, when greens were slow, but most modern greens are so quick that putting with wrists is a hazardous occupation. If you have too much wrist in the stroke, you will find it difficult to have consistent feel, especially under pressure, where your small, hand muscles are more likely to flinch and be affected than your big, shoulder muscles.

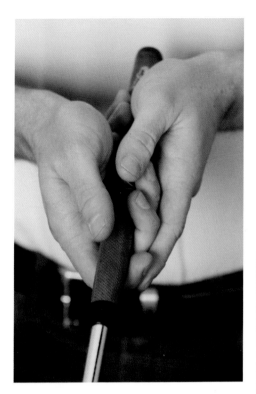

Building a good grip is the foundation of any good putting stroke.

A good grip

There has never been a good putter who grabbed the grip and throttled it as though trying to open a stuck lid on a jam jar. A good grip is a gentle grip but pressure tenses all your muscles – especially your fingers and arms. Stay loose and hold the club softly to keep your stroke rhythmical and smooth.

The aim of a good grip

The putting grip has one simple aim – to return the putterhead to the ball square to the target. Once you've achieved this, the ball will roll straight. The putting stroke is a technique in which the hands do all the work and your grip should be a unit where the hands work as one, with neither having more influence than the other.

Putterface open or closed at impact

A good grip aims to return the putterhead square at impact. If your grip is wrong, you may push or pull putts with an open or closed clubface. An open face will push them right, a closed face left. This is a result of too much hand action in the stroke, usually down to a poor grip.

Too long

Pushed putts

Pulled putts

Too short

Unusual grips

In comparison with the other techniques required to play golf to a decent level, the putting stroke is the one that is most open to interpretation and innovation. Putting is all about personal comfort. If you are comfortable with a technique that works – even though it looks ludicrous – stick with it. As a result of innovations, a variety of ways of holding the putter have evolved over the years.

The cack-handed grip

Many golfers down the years have suffered a loss of the putting stroke. A common way of rejuvenating that disappearing touch is a change of grip, and this method was invented as an alternative. The cack-handed grip suggests that, instead of putting with the left hand above the right, you place the right hand on the club first at the top of the grip with the palm facing the target. The left hand is then placed into position below the right with the back of left hand facing the target. At address the shoulders should be level with the ground making it easier to putt using a pendulum, straight-back, straight-through stroke, with the putterhead staying close to the ground throughout the shot.

The Langer grip

This weird and wonderful method helped German Bernhard Langer arrest a fall from world number one position to journeyman and the golfing doldrums. Place the left hand below the right and hold the grip tight against your left forearm, pinning it in position with the right thumb. Such a method takes hands completely out of the stroke, but it never quite established universal appeal.

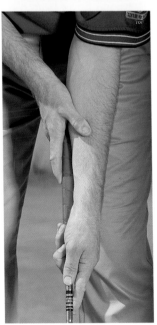

The claw

American journeyman pro Chris Dimarco raised his game to top 10 in the world through this extraordinary hold. His putting statistics went through the roof, as did his career earnings. Other tour players copied the method with varying degrees of success. Place the right hand below the left – an orthodox position – but turn the right hand over, holding the club with a claw-like grip. This technique takes out the hinge in the right wrist, leading to a smoother stroke.

Switching hands

If you are struggling on the greens and if you are one of those ambivalent golfers who has never been fully satisfied playing right-handed, don't be afraid to grab a left-handed putter from the pro-shop and see how well it goes. There are a number of successful Tour players – Notah Begay III is one – who play right-handed but putt left. The quirks and hinges of your full swing will not affect your putting stroke as a result of holding the club the other way round.

Grip basics

Whatever your grip, whichever you find most comfortable, there are common denominators with all of these techniques.

1 Hold the putter lightly. If you grip hard, you will lose all touch and become tense over the ball. Refer to the diagram. If 0 is not gripping the club at all and 10 is gripping it as tightly as possible, hold the putter with a grip rated 4.

10 too tight

Just right

0 too loose

Palm

Target line

2 Palm facing the target, back of hand facing the target. Whichever way you putt, whether it is right above left or left above right, the back of your left hand and the palm of your right face the hole, making your grip neutral and working as one solid unit.

Palm

Target line

Grips for belly and broomhandle putters

If you invest in a broomhandle or belly putter, you will not see the benefits of these modern pieces of equipment if you don't know how to use them – it would be like buying a Ferrari but only using it to trundle to the shops and back. Both longer putters have two techniques available to them.

The broomhandle grips

The two grips that are commonly used on the broomhandle putter define your stroke. Try out both these techniques and see which works better for you. There is no correct way, just the more comfortable and, of course, the more successful.

Shoulder grip

1 If you wear a watch on your left hand, use this as an indicator for your technique. Take hold of the top grip of the broomhandle putter with the watch's face pointing directly away from you – at a right angle to the target. Now your left wrist and left forearm point in a straight line towards the target.

2 The stroke produced is a rocking motion with your left shoulder as you keep your wrist, forearm and watch in line with the target. The right hand holds the club softly while steadying it through the stroke. There is little or no wrist action – the club moves purely by the motion of the shoulders.

Hand grip

1 Another broomhandle grip has your wrist stay at a right angle to the line of the putt throughout. Hold the club to the left side of your chest. Your left elbow will automatically tuck in by your side.

2 Guide the putter with your right hand and the left wrist rotating back and forwards through the stroke. Do not move the left shoulder and arm; let the right hand guide the putter.

The belly-putter grips

The controversial belly putter has driven some to success and many to distraction but there is an underlying belief that it is the safest way to putt – as long as you use the right technique. There are two reasons why the belly putter is so good. First, it takes the wrists out of the stroke. Second, it automatically makes you accelerate the clubhead through the ball. There are two grips to choose from.

The anchor

The half-broom

1 Hold the butt end of the club steadily against your belly and adopt a normal grip – reverse overlap or cack-handed.

2 Keep the butt end rigid, and the head of the putter will swing like a pendulum. Keep the end of the club still so that you produce a consistent, accelerating stroke and do not waste any movement. Your stomach becomes an anchor point that negates any unwanted movement in your hands.

1 An unorthodox way of using the belly putter: hold it like a broomhandle, split the hands so your right guides the putter while the left holds the butt end firmly against your stomach. This is the equivalent of the broomhandle's hand grip but using a belly putter.

The belly-putter debate

The problem with the belly putter is the anchor or pivot point in your stomach. Many players believe you should only touch the putter with two pivot points – your hands. By anchoring the putter in your stomach and reducing the amount of wrist in the stroke automatically, you negate the involuntary and instinctive problems of putting when under pressure. The fact that it makes the game easier and more accessible is no bad thing – but arguments will continue to rage.

THE SET-UP

Now that you have worked on a comfortable and neutral grip, addressing the ball correctly is vital in making a smooth, consistent stroke. As with the full swing, most problems within the stroke start at address, so working on the fundamentals is important.

Stance and posture

To putt well, you must be in a comfortable, stable position. Staying balanced as you rock your shoulders is key to making the ball roll smoothly, and this derives from solid posture. As you stand up straight next to the ball, try bending from your hips and letting your hands dangle naturally from your shoulders, not clamped tightly to the body. With the knees flexed and comfortable, and your back as straight and relaxed as possible, you should be in a good position.

A good set-up is a comfortable set-up.

Let your arms hang naturally from your shoulders at address.

Ball position and weight distribution

Your weight should be evenly spread across your feet at address. The stroke comes from your shoulders, not your body – an even spread will help this happen. Keep your weight on the balls of your feet, not on the heels so that you are sitting back, nor on your toes so you are toppling over. You must place the ball forward of centre in your stance as this helps you to make the ball roll end over end.

Ball position check

As ball position is vital to putting well, try this drill to make sure the ball is not slipping too far back in your stance.

As you stand in your address position with the ball in a natural place, take another ball and drop it from the bridge of your nose. It should land directly on the first ball. Alternatively, dangle your putter from your nose. If the putterhead obscures the ball on the ground, then you are in a good position. Adjust your address and keep checking this until it becomes second nature.

Making every putt straight

Putting is simple; keeping it simple is difficult. If you are struggling on greens that break and borrow, play each putt as a straight one, using good alignment. Pick a point between you and the hole where you think the break will take hold – the spot over which you want the ball to roll on its way to the hole. Now align directly to this point. Forget the hole and just play the putt as a straight putt to that specific point.

Alignment

Misalignment is the cause of most missed putts – golfers simply do not aim straight. First, the face of your putter must aim directly at the target – you are flawed from the outset if this is not the case. You want your entire body to be aligned parallel to the target line. This does not mean you should aim at the target; but imagine a line between your ball and the hole, then ensure your toes, knees, hips and – most importantly – shoulders, are all parallel to this. Place a club on the ground parallel to the target line between you and the ball. Use this as a reference in practice to ensure good alignment.

Alternative set-ups

Down the years, different players have evolved
different techniques for putting, and the broomhandle
and belly putters have cured many golfing woes. There
are, though, even more bizarre and less fashionable
techniques. Here are alternative address positions that
produce alternative strokes.

Standing open

US Tour pro Billy Mayfair has made a considerable
living through standing open to the target at address –
this means with his body aligned left. The resulting
stroke cuts across the ball-to-target line, potentially
putting sidespin on the ball and dragging it off line.
He is blessed with enormous natural touch, though,
so he manages to putt brilliantly with this somewhat
haphazard technique.

Standing closed

South African legend Bobby Locke, who won four
Open Championships, used a closed putting stance.
His stroke would then come from inside the line to
out – swung from close to his body to further away –
meaning he'd have to close the putter at impact,
making the putt 'hook'. Such overspin can make the
ball roll nicely, if started right of the target.

Knees together

When the greens around the world were not so quick,
putting strokes often contained lots of wrist and hand
action through impact, so the set-up had to reflect this.
Arnold Palmer putted for much of his career with his
knees together. The stroke was more energetic, to keep
the ball moving over the slow greens. Palmer felt more
stable with his knees together.

Crouched over the ball

Jack Nicklaus crouched over the ball throughout his illustrious career. By bending his knees and keeping his eyes rooted over the ball, he was able to judge the pace and line of the putts more accurately than his peers. Such a method restricted the rocking of the shoulders so it needed wrists and hands – not a problem on the slower greens of the 1960s.

Croquet-style

All-time legend of the game Sam Snead struggled with the yips in his later years. As a result, he pioneered the croquet-style method of putting. At address, his legs straddle the ball-to-target line as he holds the club like a croquet mallet. This method became illegal – although the reasons for its illegality are never quite clear and appear more aesthetic and traditional than anything else. It may be slightly easier to putt like this, but you still have to roll that ball into the hole.

Side-saddle

As a consequence of the banning of his croquet technique, Snead invented the next best thing – side-saddle. He stood as far down the line of the putt as he possibly could, without straddling it. Again, his chest stayed face on to the target with his hands split down the putter. As it was towards the end of the grand old man's career, the authorities let this one go.

Five keys to good set-up

Before you try any of these weird and wonderful techniques, have a go at conquering the greens with the most popular and orthodox set-up. Here are five check points to help you build solid fundamentals.

1 Ball position forward
2 Grip club softly
3 Weight on balls of feet
4 Keep eyes over the ball
5 Be comfortable

Common mistakes and their cures

Many problems on the greens come from faulty fundamentals. Here are a number of the more common difficulties that golfers have with their set-up and hints on how to overcome such troubles.

Bad posture

Putting well is all about stability. You must address the ball with good posture, so that you control your body's movement and feel comfortable over the stroke. If you hunch, you will struggle to swing freely without undue wrist action. If you stand too upright, touch and feel will desert you.

Cure: posture exercise

This is a simple exercise that you can do at any time, whether you have a ball and club to hand or not.

1 First, stand upright, above what would be the ball. Then let your arms hang naturally, as though you are holding a putter. Stand with your back as straight as possible.

2 Now bend from your hips and your hips only. Keep your arms dangling naturally from your shoulders until the point at which the putter would touch the ground. Concentrate on tilting over your belt buckle, keeping your back and legs straight.

3 Finally, flex your knees slightly so you are comfortable and let your bottom stick out while keeping your back straight. You should feel stable, solid and comfortable.

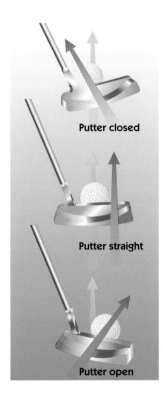

Putter closed

Putter straight

Putter open

Poor alignment

If you are unable to align your body parallel to the ball-to-target line, you are less likely to putt straight with a simple pendulum stroke. Often golfers will stand closed (aligned right) or open (aligned left) of the target, which is fine if you are blessed with natural touch and flair; usually doing this makes life more difficult and leads to inconsistent putts.

Cure: use short putts

The best way to drill natural and good alignment into your putting is through making a series of short putts. Give yourself 1.2 metre (4 ft), 1.5 metre (5 ft) and 1.8 metre (6 ft) putts on a flat area. To constrain yourself, place two clubs on the ground on either side of your ball aimed directly towards the hole, then use another club along your toe line set parallel to the clubs around the ball. Accurate alignment becomes natural after hitting a number of short putts like this.

Three drills for better set-up

Many problems in the putting stroke originate from a poor address position, so here are four quick practices that will help you in the set-up. Keep an eye on all of these, especially if you have played a lot. When you are playing, it is easy to get into lazy habits and let the fundamentals slip, leading to an inexplicable loss of form on the greens.

Ball position 1

Ball position is vital when putting. The ball must be forward in your stance and you need to have your eyes over it. If your eyes are inside or outside the line of the putt, it becomes difficult to judge the line. Imagine you are rolling the ball at the hole underarm. Would you swing your arm to the side of your body or from close to under your nose? The further to the side, the more difficult it is to aim so you would try to keep your arm as close to the ball-to-target line as possible.

Ball position 2

Similarly, when you putt, your eyes need to be over the line of the ball to give you a decent perspective and proper feel for the shot. To help maintain a decent ball position, stand to the ball as normal, take another ball and place it by your left eye. Let the one by your eye drop – if your position is good, it will land straight on the ball on the ground. Keep practising until this becomes natural.

Using a mirror

Drilling your address position in a mirror or in your reflection is one of the best ways to spend 20 minutes. Find a full-length reflection – many driving ranges these days will provide such facilities – and address a ball as though you are putting at the mirror. Look at your reflection – how is your posture? Is your head over the line of the ball? Do you look athletic and solid or slouched and weak? Run through the posture drills to make a decent address become second nature.

Stay connected

Keeping your arms and chest linked together is as important for a putting stroke as for the full swing. As soon as your arms and chest lose the connection, your wrist and forearms come into play, which creates inconsistency and problems. Whenever you address the ball, allow your arms to hang naturally from your shoulders. If you turn your hands so their backs are opposite your thighs, with your palms facing out and elbows turned in, then turn your hands to face each other, your arms, chest and shoulders will feel well-linked and a solid unit. After that, you can take hold of your putter and concentrate on making practice strokes, using your shoulders to rock the putter back and forth – your big, consistent muscles are in control.

THE STROKE

The standard putting stroke has changed over the years. Nowadays, with modern equipment and quick greens, putting is a different prospect from when the greens were as quick as mud and the putters were bits of metal stuck on the end of wooden shafts. Here are the basic principles of a solid stroke.

The simple stroke

1 Do not let any part of your body move that doesn't need to move – this is one of the keys to putting. This is a stroke that comes entirely from the shoulders rocking back and through. Any extra movement from your hands, wrists, forearms or body will knock your stroke off line.

2 Try not to keep your hands and arms rigid and stiff as this will compromise your touch in the stroke. Keep them as flexible and loose as possible. You are looking for the club to swing like a pendulum from your shoulders – back and through – smoothly and easily.

3 Accelerate through the ball at impact – otherwise you will have a hesitant and stabbing stroke. Your throughswing should be as long as your backswing, with all the energy coming from your shoulders, not your arms or body. Stay relaxed and comfortable through the stroke or you'll become jerky.

Staying on line

  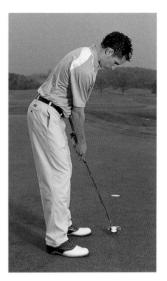

1 Move your putter back directly on the ball-to-target line, with only your shoulders rocking. If any movement from your hands creeps into the shot, you will misdirect your putterface. Concentrate on keeping your arms and body linked throughout – working together and not against each other.

2 Impact is the moment of truth. In reality, it does not matter how you have made the putter arrive at this point – all you need is the face to be square to the ball-to-target line, irrespective of where it has travelled before. That said, if you take the putter back on line, it will be much easier to return it accurately and consistently.

3 Keep your rhythm and tempo the same throughout the stroke, leading to a smooth acceleration at impact and beyond. This is what positive putting is all about. Making sure you do not truncate your follow-through will help keep that tempo even and avoid a stuttering stroke.

Putting stroke checklist

• Take putter back on the line of the putt as this increases your chances of returning it square to the ball at impact.

• Use only shoulders in the stroke; no body, arms or legs – the big muscles in your shoulders will keep your stroke both solid and consistent.

• Keep the connection between arms and body throughout, because once the connection has been lost so has the control of the clubhead.

• Accelerate through the ball at the point of impact to avoid uneven tempo and jerky strokes.

The putter paths

As with many of the techniques in golf, there are no hard and fast rules for the correct putter path. There are firm guidelines, there are suggested movements, but, when it comes down to it, if it works for you there is no need to change. So, when putting, there are two distinct types of stroke that you can choose between and that you can develop yourself.

Many think the basic movement below is the most reliable and simplest way to putt – nothing can go wrong, the putterface aims directly at the target throughout and it is a simple concept to understand.

Straight back, straight through

1 Swing the putter like a steady pendulum, straight back then straight through. As the putter comes back, it points directly at the line of the hole.

2 Once the putter swings through, it continues down the target line, encouraging the ball on to the correct path. There is no 'hit' as the club makes contact with the ball; contact is purely incidental to that perfect pendulum stroke because the ball gets in the way of the shot, leading to a pure and perfect roll.

Suit yourself
If you play with a straight back, straight through stroke – or square to square technique – then a face-balanced head is more suitable and will give you a better roll. If your stroke is inside the line to square, then a heel-toe putter is more applicable. Find what suits your stroke and what you feel most comfortable with – comfort is the most important element when choosing a putter.

Inside the line to square path

1 Take the club back inside the line, which will cause the putter to swing closer to your body as you take it away, instead of staying directly on line with the putt. This small difference will mean that the putter does not stay on the target line throughout.

2 Once the putter returns to the ball at impact, it is square to the target line, creating a pure roll. This technique is often used over longer putts where an extended backswing automatically pulls the club inside the line. Many golfers feel it is a natural way to putt; think of a door swinging and the path the edge of the door takes as it swings in a smooth, even arc rather than a straight line – the analogy holds true for putting.

Advantages of each technique

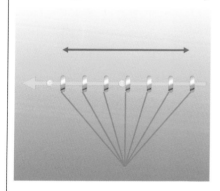

Straight back, straight through
- Putterface always aiming at the target.

- Easy to understand and reliable, simple technique.

- Easy to control tempo, ball 'gets in way' of swing.

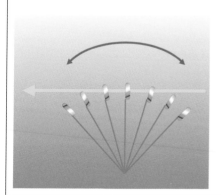

Inside the line to square path
- Natural way to putt; putter naturally swings in arc.

- Simple over longer putts as club automatically swings inside line.

- Often a comfortable action to make.

Common mistakes – easy cures

Here are three common mistakes you will see on any putting green on a Saturday morning. The cures are simple but do require time to take full effect. No one has ever become a great putter overnight. You may find a new club or tip works in the short term, but for long-term improvement practice is the only way.

Uneven tempo

An even tempo and good rhythm are essential when putting. If you see jerky strokes or stuttering follow-throughs, tempo and rhythm have broken down. The backswing has become too long or too short, and the golfer has to compensate by either decelerating the club towards impact or hitting through the ball harder. Short backswings lead to a stiff jab at the ball and long backswings lead to a painful hesitation at impact.

Cure: improve your backswing

1 Stand about 6 metres (20 ft) from the hole and drop three balls on the ground. Concentrate on making a very short backswing but still try to hole the putt. What happens? You have to jab at the ball, your technique breaks down and you have little control.

2 Now hit the next ball with an exaggeratedly long backswing – how easy is it to get close consistently? You have to slow down through impact and may well catch some grass as well as the ball.

3 Finally, make a stroke with an in-between length of backswing – you will suddenly find it easier and more accurate, keeping that tempo even and solid.

Wrist breaker

To putt consistently, you need to rely on your big muscles which are strong and difficult to move out of line. Your shoulder and back muscles are

unlikely to suffer involuntary twitches or twist at an unwanted time. A common problem is excess wrist in the putting stroke. Your wrists must be quiet throughout, not rigid and stiff, but firm and stable.

Cure: use a pen

To avoid this problem, slip a pen down the back of your glove before you putt. Make some medium-length putts of 2–3 m (6–10 feet), letting the pen act as a splint to hold your wrist in place. This gives a feeling of driving the back of your

left hand towards the hole which is vital for a smooth stroke. If you collapse your wrists in the stroke, the pen will jab your hand, giving a warning of technique breakdown!

Swing paths

If you are struggling to hit putts straight, you could be taking the club too far inside or outside the line.

If you take the club outside the line (see below middle), you are liable to cut across the ball, causing sidespin. This can drag the ball offline.

Similarly, if you approach the putt from inside the line too much (see below left), you could end up pushing it right.

Place a ball next to a wall. Address it normally so your eyes are over the ball and rest your head against the wall. Now practise stroking smoothly, keeping

the putterhead away from, but parallel to the bottom of the wall. As you practise avoiding the wall, you will develop a consistent back and through stroke.

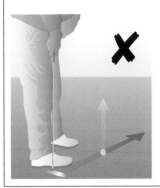

Smoothing out that stroke

Putting is the most important part of the game, yet it is the one most ignored by amateur golfers when they go to the practice range. Putting practice can be tedious but a few simple drills can liven up the experience. Here are four simple drills to help your stroke – the fundamental technique.

The push drill

To help check your putter aim and your swing path, try this unorthodox drill: find a flat putt of about 1 metre (3 ft) long. As you address the ball, set the clubface square with your toes and body aligned parallel to the ball-to-target line. Instead of taking the usual backswing, brush the ball into the hole by pushing it forwards firmly. If the ball rolls into the centre of the hole and drops, your alignment is good and your swing path comes through square. If you missed it left, you could be pulling putts or aiming left of the target. If it missed right, pushes or inaccuracy could be the problem. You can now iron out these basic technique problems by keeping the basics accurate.

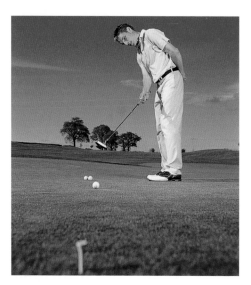

One-handed practice

To help with the free flow and smooth acceleration of your putting stroke, spend 20 minutes on the putting green making putts with just your bottom hand. Keep your top hand in your pocket or behind your back, so it is completely out of the way, hold the club gently and concentrate on the flow of the swing, letting the putterhead gently move through the ball. You will get good at this quickly.

Ball between the wrists

If you are struggling with consistency in length, you may be using too much wrist in your stroke. Try this to overcome difficulties. Address the ball and place another ball between your wrists at the end of your grip. Hit putts with this ball in place, making sure it does not drop. Any unwanted wrist movement will make it move, so your wrists must be still in order to hold it in place.

Empty bottle practice

Keeping your body and arms working in unison is central to putting well. If your shoulders and arms are out of synch, you will have a staccato and inconsistent stroke. Place an empty water bottle between your left arm and your side, holding it in place. Now address the ball and make some putts.

As you swing back, make sure the water bottle does not drop; keep holding it firmly. This will immediately keep your stroke on line as the bottle will drop if you take the club too much inside or outside the line. You must not become wooden in your stroke but it is vital to have a solid framework around which to build your technique. So don't grip it too tightly – just firmly.

Good practice

- Practise putting with the balls you will use for real – each ball has a different feel so get used to the ones you'll be using.

- Loosen your back before putting, as this can become sore.

- Only practise putting over straight putts, to avoid your stroke compensating for slopes.

- Only practise until you have had enough; don't force extra hours out of it just for the sake of it – this will not achieve anything.

PUTTING PREPARATION

Your manner and method of approaching a putt is vital in attaining consistent success on the greens. If you develop a solid routine, good etiquette and know-how on the putting surface, you will grow in confidence. A confident and smart putter will intimidate opponents and sink more putts.

Arrive prepared

As soon as you walk on to the green, know where you need to go to read the putt accurately. Look at the green as you approach it and start developing a sense of the slopes, pace and landscape of the green. Read the putt while your opponent plays so you are prepared and quick when it comes to your turn.

Mark the ball properly

Many golfers do not mark the ball properly. It is always worth marking and cleaning your ball – any lump of mud on the side of the ball can cause it to veer sideways, leading to missed putts. Make sure you place the marker behind the ball – not between the ball and the hole. If you place the marker in front of the ball, an opponent may think you are stealing a few centimetres when you replace the ball. Also, if you mark in front of your ball, you will then have to putt over the hole your marker has made in the putting surface. After marking, give the ball a good wipe before replacing it. This cleaning process ought to ensure a pure strike and roll.

Cleaning your ball before you putt will ensure a pure roll.

Place the marker on the opposite side of the ball to the hole.

When arriving on the green

- Read putt as you approach the green.

- Look for pitchmarks to repair.

- Mark and clean your ball.

- Replace ball, run through pre-putt routine, then make the putt.

Read the putt

Reading the putt accurately is essential for holing regularly – this is not in doubt. Many golfers waste time by being ill-prepared and uncertain. If you are confident with your read, go ahead and play – second-guessing can lead to doubt and hesitant strokes. It is frustrating for playing partners, opponents and fellow golfers if each putt takes too long to read, so develop a quick and sensible routine for reading putts and stick to it.

Pitchmark repair

One of the duties all golfers have is the upkeep of the course. This means not only replacing divots on the fairway but also repairing pitchmarks on the green. Never repair one pitchmark, always find a second and repair that as well. If all golfers do this, a green holds its quality for longer and your putts are less likely to get knocked off line by an unwanted crater on the putting surface.

Jargon buster

'Pitchmark' A pitchmark is a hole on a green made by the ball when it lands. Depending on the softness and type of the green, any ball landing on the green from any distance is liable to make a mark and this needs repairing.

Top tip

If you are putting from off the green, you are entitled to leave the flag in the hole. Many golfers prefer to have it taken out, thinking it improves their chances of the ball dropping. This is wrong. Putting guru Dave Pelz spent hours rolling thousands of balls at holes with flags both in and out, and found conclusive proof that you are more likely to hole the putt with the flag in than with it out.

Repairing pitchmarks is an important responsibility for everybody on the course.

Green rules and etiquette

Golf is a game of rules and strict etiquette that helps golfers play safely, enjoyably and fairly. On the green, the etiquette and rules are stricter, which is unsurprising considering it is the business end of the game.

Rules

Repair pitchmarks not spikemarks

Before you putt, you are allowed to repair any pitchmarks on the green but you must not repair spikemarks or any other damage on the green prior to playing. If you do repair any damage that has been made by anything other than a ball before you play, you lose the hole in matchplay and incur a two-stroke penalty in strokeplay. You are not allowed to make any repairs to the green if you are not on it – this mistake is often made when a golfer is playing from the fringe.

Don't hit the flag

If you are on the green, you will suffer a two-stroke penalty if your ball strikes the flag when it is in the hole (rule 17-3). Whenever you are on the putting surface, make sure either your partner tends the flag or it is taken out. You are allowed to putt with it in, as long as you don't strike it.

Striking your opponent's ball with your ball

This is an awkward situation and is best resolved by always marking your ball when an opponent is playing. The ball that has been hit must be replaced as near as possible to its original position. The other ball is played where it finishes, which could be better or worse as this depends on the rub of the green. There is no penalty for this.

You are not allowed to repair spikemarks on the line of your putt, only pitchmarks.

If you strike your opponent's ball, you may get a lucky break and finish close.

Etiquette

Where do I stand?

You must never stand directly behind your playing partner or opponent when they are putting. Not only is this extremely irritating for the person who is playing, you are gaining an unfair advantage by having a good look at the break on the putt – and so is against the rules.

Never stand directly behind your opponent or partner when they are putting – this is against the rules of the game.

How do I move around the green?

Never walk across the line of someone else's putt; that is the only rule. If you are tapping the ball in from a few centimetres, make sure you are not standing across the line of another's putt. Although this piece of etiquette is increasingly redundant thanks to rubber cleats on golf shoes that leave no marks on the putting surface, it is still important to follow because walking across another golfer's line shows a lack of regard for them.

Where do I cast my shadow?

Again, cast your shadow anywhere but across the line of another player's putt or the hole. This can become an issue early in the day or later in the evening when the sun is lower, so be aware of it when you are playing at these times. If your shadow is across the line of a putt, it can be difficult to judge the line and pace of the putt.

If in doubt, offer to tend the flag for your opponent or playing partner.

When do I tend the flag?

Offer to tend the flag for your partner or opponent at all reasonable times – if they are playing a longer putt and may not be able to make out the hole clearly. Many golfers prefer to have the pin out at all times; in this case, you should remove it.

The pre-putt routine

The final part of preparing for a putt is the most important one, especially when it comes to dealing with pressure. Developing a regular and consistent pre-putt routine is essential in making the most of decent technique as it will stop your stroke breaking down when the heat is on.

The brain and hands work better if they are reacting to a situation rather than consciously thinking about the task ahead. This basic routine makes putting reactive, by keeping you moving and by training your brain to pick up the pace and line without having to think.

All about timing

Your routine must always take the same time, from your first look at the situation to pulling the trigger. Take Tiger Woods – for each putt he plays in whatever situation, whether it is to force a play-off in a Major or a 1 metre (3 ft) putt on the first hole of the week at a run-of-the-mill tournament, his routine takes as long. Amateurs often take a short time over standard putts and far too long over the crucial, crunch putts. You need consistency if you want to be a consistently good putter. It is something to fall back on under pressure.

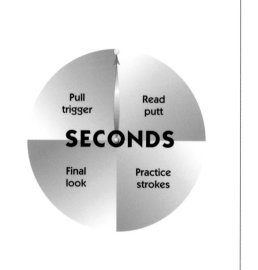

Reading the putt

You will always take a general look at the lie of the land as you approach the green. Next, crouch behind the ball and picture the path you want your ball to take. Imagine it rolling and try to get a feel for the weight of the ball and for the momentum it requires over the distance it has to travel.

Rehearsals

Make a gentle waggle of the putter as you are approaching the ball to feel the putterhead gently swinging in your hands. This rehearses the feel of the putt. You have already gleaned information on line and distance in your head. Now you have to put this into your hands.

The correct approach

You do not want to approach the ball from directly behind the ball-to-target line – unless it is a dead straight putt. Walk towards the putt on the line on which you intend to start the ball. Arrive at the ball from the correct angle to give yourself an accurate perspective on the putt.

Practise swinging

Make your practice strokes while looking at the hole. Stand over the ball, look at the hole and make two or three strokes, keeping your eye on the target. Make your practice strokes long and smooth – long enough to ensure the ball reaches the hole. This must be the stroke you will use for real.

Pulling the trigger

Put the putter behind the ball and line it up to the starting point. Then double-check it. Look at the hole once, draw your head back over the ball and pull the trigger. Stop over the ball for only a fraction of a second. You must not freeze on the putt. You have done the hard work, so trust your read and preparation and putt positively.

THE SHORT PUTT

If you can consistently, confidently and without even noticing it hole from 3 metres (10 ft) and closer – as we all should be able to – you will reduce your handicap by six. Not only do missed short putts cost immediately, they also put pressure on your short game to get even closer, leading to hesitant chipping. This section talks about specific techniques and practices for nailing those frustrating ones regularly.

The basic stroke

1 The fundamentals are the same for a short putt as for a longer one. Hold the putter in the same way, address the ball in the same way – in fact any changes you make will increase your chances of missing the putt. Your approach is different, however. For 90 per cent of all short putts you must not aim outside the hole. You are trying to hole out, so always take dead aim.

2 To make a confident stroke and clean strike, maintain your rhythm and tempo – you have to swing the club at the same pace as you would for a longer putt. The only difference is the length of your backswing – it will be much shorter. Your putter still swings straight back and straight through like a pendulum.

3 As before, accelerate through the ball. For a short putt, this is essential as you are more likely to be hesitant because of the added pressure – you are expected to hole out, so the fear of failure is greater. Swing positively through to a long finish, letting the ball become incidental to your stroke.

How to make a positive stroke

To help make a positive stroke, try to forget about the ball and think of your clubhead instead. Keep your eyes on the club as it swings back and have only one thought in your mind. Look to cover the hole with the putter's head. This will instantly force you to swing positively as well as down the line of the putt. You will find it difficult to underhit putts if you are using this technique.

Listen to the drop

When you are over a short putt, keep looking at where the ball was until you hear the rattle in the bottom of the cup. Nick Faldo was a great exponent of listening to the drop; even over the final metre (3 ft) putt to win Majors he'd never see the ball go in the hole. This technique keeps your body steady and still over a tricky distance that exposes any flaws in your stroke.

Half back, double through

Hitting short putts firmly is essential. The more firm the stroke, the less you need to worry about the break. If you strike short putts solidly, you can aim directly at the back of the hole. To help with this, make your backswing half as long as your follow-through. You can practise this by placing a tee about 5 cm (2 inches) behind your ball at address. Only swing the club far enough back to hit the tee. This will force you to accelerate through the impact.

Take the putter back half the length as you swing through.

Coping with the yips

The yips is the most debilitating problem on the golf course and the cause of much frustration and golfing depression. It can strike anyone from the best golfer in the world to the newest beginner. If you have never heard of the yips before, you are lucky. When faced with a short putt, the golfer inexplicably flinches at the ball, with a spasmodic flick of the wrists. The stroke is involuntary and the ball is out of control, often finishing far from the hole.

On-course cure

Bernhard Langer has defeated the yips three times. He has managed it through working exceptionally hard on the putting green and relying on a great all-round game to piece together scores. The biggest change he made may work for you – change your grip. Whether it is a reverse-overlap or cack-handed grip, just try the opposite of what is normal. Make your body use different muscles for the same job – this can work in the short term and may be a longer-term cure.

The yips is a debilitating problem that can ruin your game, round and love of the sport.

Jargon buster

'The yips' A disabling 'condition' that can reduce a world-beater to the status of a handicap golfer and give grown men nervous breakdowns. Short putts seem huge, leading to an involuntary flick at the ball. The communication between the brain and hands breaks down, leaving golfers riddled with nerves and, in extreme cases, unable even to take the club back.

Longer-term cures

To rid yourself of the yips you need to spend serious hours on the practice green. Here are three drills to help.

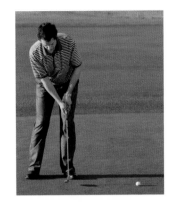

Focus on the line

Focus more on seeing the line and feeling the distance of the putt rather than on technique. Look at the hole and not the putterhead when making practice strokes; then, as you hit the putt, keep your eyes firmly fixed on the exact spot where the ball was when the putterface struck.

Hear success

To help overcome the yips, avoid any practice with pressure such as holing 100 short putts in a row – you need nursing not punishing. Hit short putts with your eyes closed, to enjoy the sound of the ball rattling in the bottom of the cup. You won't be able to see the moment of impact, which will give you greater freedom through impact.

Keep it simple

There can only be two outcomes to a putt. It will go in or you will miss. Try to keep your thought-process simple. You can keep it even simpler by taking the target away altogether and concentrating on your strike alone. Putt either to a tee-peg or to a coin on the ground, or nothing at all – take the consequences away from your actions and start to get into the groove of a confident technique.

Yips – the history

Many of the greatest golfers have suffered this ignoble and severe problem. It is a real disorder, like a disease, and there is ongoing research in the United States trying to work out the cause. They are getting closer to a breakthrough and they believe it is a cross between repetitive strain injury and a psychological problem. One thing is certain; it requires heavy putting-green time to cure, but it can be overcome.

Essential short-putt practice

As with any part of the game, your ability to hole regularly from close range comes down to how much you practise from this distance. Here are some simple and effective ways to make holing from 3 metres (10 ft) and closer become second nature.

The compass drill

Place four balls 1 metre (3 ft) away from the hole at the points of the compass and, as you move around the hole, you sink each putt. Once you have done this successfully, place the balls 1.8 metres (6 ft) from the hole. Again, you can try to sink each ball in turn. If you miss, set up the balls once again and continue until you have sunk four consecutively.

Keep pushing the balls back as far as you can, trying to break your distance record each time. The practice is effective because it drills four different breaks for the same distance of putt – how often do you have a completely straight short putt? It shows that you rarely need to aim outside the hole.

Spot putt

To develop a firm strike over shorter lengths, give yourself a straight 1.8 metre (6 ft) putt and place a tee-peg in the back of the hole. Aim to hit this tee-peg in the back of the hole, as opposed to dribbling the ball over the front edge. Pick that specific and small point and nail the putt directly at it. If you miss by a tiny fraction, the ball will still drop. When you are on the course, use this technique by imagining the tee-peg at the back of the hole, or picking a mark or piece of grass in the cup.

The tennis-ball drill

A fantastic method of instantly building confidence over this length is to practise putting with a tennis ball. To hole a 3 metre (10 ft) putt with a tennis ball you have to strike the middle of the ball and make it drop in the centre of the hole. Now putt with a real golf ball – the hole will seem vast and the ball tiny, just what you need to hole short putts. Practise like this for 10 minutes before teeing off and that illusion of a bucket-type hole will remain with you.

Shaft practice

If your short putts are endlessly coming up short or just breaking past the hole, dying away just before the hole, then you are not striking the ball positively enough. Remember, as the ball runs out of energy it takes more of the break. The firmer the strike, the less you have to worry about any slopes. To become more positive, lay a club in front of the hole, then knock in three short putts over this club. You will have to strike firmly to jump the shaft.

Making 100 putts

Building consistency under pressure is key to holing short putts regularly. A fantastic, if time-consuming, method of practising pressure putts is to attempt to hole 100 short putts consecutively. If you miss, you must go back to zero. Start with unmissable putts – from immediately beside the hole – in order to build your confidence and then move to tricky 1 metre (3 ft) ones.

Short-putt psychology

You should hole every short putt – you can hole every short putt. Everyone knows this; which is why that length is so tough. Fear of failure is at its greatest. In other words, most problems over short putts are in your head. Here are simple ways to think and approach those pressure-fuelled short putts.

Before the round

Build confidence before the round by heading to the putting green, but use the time constructively and not simply to idle away 20 minutes before your tee time.

Take three balls with you and give yourself a short putt. Hole each of the three balls from this distance

Concentrate on the sensations of the ball rattling in the bottom of the cup and coming off the middle of the club. Do this three times, then move back to 1.8 metres (6 ft). When you have completed a set, return to the shorter distance and hole three more before moving to the tee.

Strokeplay putting in matchplay

When you play strokeplay, you have to hole every putt. In matchplay your opponent can concede short putts that are, in theory, impossible to miss. Tactics dictate that your opponent will not give you all the putts you might expect. So, in matchplay, approach the round as strokeplay and expect to hole out. Remember, if you think a putt should be conceded then by definition it is impossible to miss – so what is the problem with having to putt?

Holing short putts consistently is about confidence and you build this through practice and preparation.

Walking the walk

If you are twitchy over shorter putts, your body language will give this away. It is simple to spot a golfer who lacks confidence over the nerve janglers. Approaching the putt with a tense mind will not help you hole out and walking nervously towards it, will add to this terror.

To help you think positively over short putts, walk as though you mean it. Striding confidently over to the ball, chest out, and an inward smile can trick your mind into feeling confident and positive, despite what is going on within. If you look the way you want to feel, you eventually do feel that way.

Stick to your routine

A common mistake made by amateur golfers is to approach short and crunch putts differently to others. Short putts require the care and attention of a longer putt, but no more than that. Treat them as normal, make your pre-putt routine last the same time as it would for any other putt – not longer or shorter.

Short-putt tips

- Be positive and firm with your stroke, taking the break out of the putt.

- Never aim outside the hole.

- Make your follow-through double the length of your backswing.

- Accelerate through the ball.

- Listen to the rattle of the ball in the hole.

- Walk and think in a positive manner.

THE LONG PUTT

Putting well from distance will save you shots when you are not striking the ball as sweetly with your approach shots as you would like. Avoiding three-putts is essential when you are building a score – three-putts are often caused by careless putting rather than a treacherous green – regular two-putts keep the momentum of the round going, lift your spirits and help you attack pins without fear of dropping shots uselessly.

The basic stroke

1 Again, the technique for longer putts is the same as for any other putt. Keeping the mechanics of your stroke consistent and regular is essential if you are to make decent contact and produce a pure roll. Concentrate on alignment and on knowing exactly where you are aiming. As this will be a more energetic stroke, good posture is vital to keep you stable and balanced through the shot.

2 The main difference in the stroke is the length of your backswing. Control the length of the putt with the length of the backswing – the longer the putt, the further you take the club back. This is the only adjustment you should make for longer putts. It is essential to keep your tempo and rhythm whatever the distance, so that you are always accelerating through impact.

3 The length of your throughswing must match the length of your backswing. This will ensure you accelerate through the ball and will help you keep that tempo even throughout. Swing down the line of the putt, making your putterhead follow the ball's line in the few seconds after impact.

Pace not line

If you have ever seen amateur golfers spending hours reading a long putt, working out what the ball will do over every section of its 18 metre (60 ft) course, then they are making a mistake by concentrating on the wrong aspect of the putt. Putting successfully from distance is all about pace, judgement and control.

Break comes into it but only on a general basis. The break over the first 4.5 metres (15 ft) is irrelevant as the ball will travel fast over this and it won't take effect. For an informative read, look at the last 3 metres (10 ft) of the putt, where the ball will lose pace and the break will take effect – this is the business end of the shot.

Every putt is straight

When you are lining up your putt, pick a spot between the hole and your ball and align everything to this, as though you are playing a straight putt. Break each putt down in your mind so that it becomes a straight putt, keeping the shot and the read simple and easy to line up.

Aim for the barrel

When you are putting from distance, imagine a barrel of water sunk just beneath the flag – forming a circle around its base. Aim to leave your ball anywhere in the barrel. This circle is a no-miss zone, so if your ball finishes within it you'll be facing a tap-in as opposed to a tricky short putt to save par.

Long-putt problems and solutions

Many problems with putting from distance are rooted in technical breakdown. The more energetic, longer stroke has more chance of going wrong, leading to a poor strike, which makes it difficult to obtain pace and direction – not a good mix if you are looking to avoid three-putts. Here are a number of tips that will sharpen your ball striking and encourage better control.

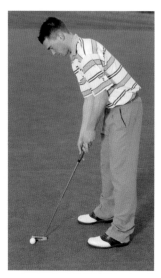

Regular mishitting

Often golfers will have great judgement of pace and line but from time to time it appears to break down. This is often down to a poor strike – the ball has to come off the middle of the club to make that decent judgement count for anything. Excessive lower body movement – a common mistake, frequently causes mishits when the stroke is longer.

Cure:
watch the coin

To avoid lower body movement you need to keep your head down. This is a bad idea for the full swing but important for putting. When you are next practising, place a coin underneath your ball and putt. As the ball moves from its original position, keep looking at the coin beneath and not the ball. Practise until this becomes second

nature. You cannot place a coin under the ball during a round but you can maintain this principle of keeping your head down.

Struggling to judge distance

Have you ever looked at a putt and been unable to make out how far it is? You can see your ball and the hole but you cannot make out the distance between the two – the green is bland, the sky is grey and there seems to be no definition to the shot. You are looking at a blank canvas and cannot judge the distance.

Cure: tend the flag

Such a problem is caused by the lack of detail in the 'picture' of the putt. There are no details giving you perspective of distance. A simple answer is to ask your partner or opponent to tend the flag, instantly adding depth and focus to the shot and making distances easier to judge.

Hitting not stroking

Over longer distances, it is easy to try to hit the putt harder. You are keen to get the ball up to the hole and you know you need to add power to the shot. The result can be a loss of tempo and a jerking hit, as opposed to a smooth stroke through the ball.

Cure: hover your club

A simple aid to this problem is to hover the putter at address. Take your normal address position, holding the club gently, but lift it a tiny fraction off the ground before you putt. Make practice strokes from this position, feeling the smoothness and freedom of the technique, especially as you take the club away.

Essential long-putt practice

Practising long-distance putts can be a thankless task; most of the putts are unlikely to drop. In effect, you are rehearsing failure – so you must carefully work out specific practice drills for this length to help your technique and avoid a creeping sense of hopelessness through endlessly missing. Here are drills and thoughts that will help your technique and approach.

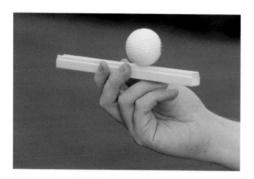

The tube drill

This drill will help you overcome too much lower-body movement. You need to find a piece of plastic or tubing about 20 cm (8 inches) long and make a slice down the side so that a ball can rest in the ridge when held horizontally. When you take your putting address, place the tubing firmly between your knees while you put a ball in the centre on the ridge.

Now putt and concentrate on the ball staying on the piece of plastic or tubing. If you have too much lower-body movement it will drop or slide. If your lower body is steady, the ball will stay balanced and you'll be solid from this distance.

Count the holes like Tiger

One of the few statistics that Tiger Woods remembers is the number of consecutive holes he has played without three-putting. This boosts his confidence and builds a great library of positive putting memories. Believe it or not, there have been stretches over which he has played 200 tournament holes without a three-putt. He acknowledges this as a crucial thought that gives him a lift, adds sharpness and improves concentration.

Don't putt to a hole

To help build confidence and to avoid that sense of never holing out when you are practising, don't putt to a hole all the time. Hit towards a tee-peg stuck in the practice green or a towel laid out flat. If you switch between these two, you will become less result-orientated in your practice and, instead, will concentrate on feel. Switching from an unspecific target to a specific target adds variety to your practice that also improves touch. As you are never holing a putt, you are never missing either – so you naturally become more confident with your technique and your touch.

Gateway drill

To improve your ball striking, which is vital in developing accurate judgement of pace, pin two tees either side of the ball at address, so they form a gateway for you to hit through. While you make some putts, make sure that you are striking the backs of the tees crisply. Trap the ball and the tees at the same time so the putterface always makes flush contact. To help keep your lower body still, keep your eyes on the tees once you have made contact.

Don't think too hard!

Becoming too conscious about long putts can cause all sorts of problems. If you are struggling over this longer distance, try and blank your mind of everything and not think about the shot in front of you – just let your instincts take over. This was Justin Rose's tactic in his resurgent 2002 season – don't think, just putt.

Be the grandfather clock

Your putting motion should be like a pendulum – but think of it as a pendulum in a grandfather clock, where your body is the casing. The pendulum swings but the case doesn't move. Your shoulders and putter swing; the rest of your body is still and stable.

Long-putt psychology

To drive your handicap down, consistency from distance is a must. If you fail regularly to leave yourself easy second putts, the ball will never have a chance of dropping. Holing a smattering of long putts recovers mistakes and saves shots as well as lifting your confidence. Here are simple thoughts and procedures that will help longer putts drop.

Warming up properly will give you a decent feel for the pace of the greens and will cut down three-putts.

Before the round

Head to the putting green with the aim of gauging the speed of the greens so you can hit the ground running once you reach the first. Take three balls, place them on the green and make one 6 metre (20 ft) putt, but don't aim at anything. Try to hit that first ball with your second and third balls, working solely on the pace of the putt.

Once you have made the three shots, putt them back to where you started, repeating the process. You will quickly gain a feel for the green. Before you head to the tee, knock three short putts into the hole to give you a positive feeling of holing out.

Become the artist

Distance putting gives you scope to express the artistic side of your game. Relish and enjoy the challenge of developing and showing accurate touch. From range, putting is all about pace and judging pace is all about feel as opposed to mechanics. Try to live and breathe the putt; close your eyes to imagine the putt rolling close and dropping. Become creative; let yourself go when working on your touch shots.

Basic psychology

If I tell you not to think of a pink elephant, what do you do immediately? That pink elephant pops into your head. It doesn't matter whether you are trying to avoid the thought, that it is mentioned at all leads to its appearance in your mind.

Similarly, when you are over a long putt, you don't need any destructive thoughts in your mind. Saying to yourself, 'Come on, don't three-putt' is more likely to make you three-putt, as this negative thought is already knocking around your brain.

So, instead of worrying over what you don't want to do, tell yourself what you do want to achieve: 'Knock this dead' or, better still, 'This one's going in'. By thinking positively, you will in turn act positively and have improved results.

Give yourself positive encouragement – tell yourself what you want to do.

Hole every putt

In the late 1990s, the women's game became flooded by a series of highly talented golfers from Scandinavia such as Annika Sorenstam. What made them so great was their aggression and positive attitude. Their coaches encouraged them to ignore two-putts and to try to hole every putt. Add this approach to your game and maybe you can achieve world domination like Annika.

Long-putt keys

● Pace is essential over long putts – line is secondary.

● Control pace of putt with length of backswing.

● Practise at specific and non-specific targets.

● Avoid practising to miss.

IMPROVING TOUCH

Jargon buster

'Pace of greens' How far the ball rolls when it is putted. If the ball rolls far for a soft putt this is a quick green and vice versa.

Arriving on a green and being surprised by how slow or quick it is can cost you shots. There are clues and hints around the course that give you an idea of pace before you putt. Look for the signs on every hole as the speed of the putting surfaces will vary over 18 holes.

Gauging the green

Golf courses are tricky places. Designers use the contours of the land to entice you into making a wrong decision and playing the wrong shot. This is always true on the greens. If you think your putt is flat, take five seconds to check your surroundings. Is the hole on a hill or slope? If the answer is yes to both of these, then you have clues. If you are putting towards a fairway that slopes away from you, you probably have a downhill putt even if the green seems flat.

Looking for clues

● **The colour of the green:** light greens are often quicker than darker greens.

● **Bare patches:** dry patches will make the putt quicker; wet ones slow it down.

● **Overhanging trees:** these often cause bare patches. When they surround the green, pay careful attention, especially as this putting surface will be different from greens on the same course that are more open to the elements.

Learning about the pace of different types of greens is essential in putting consistently.

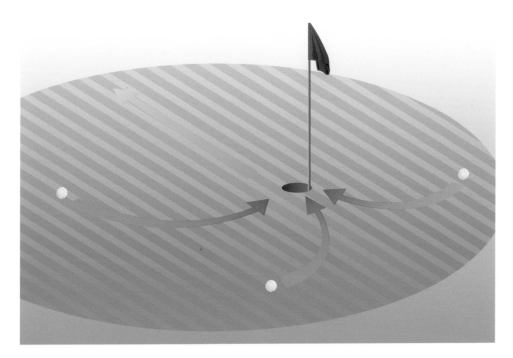

Take time to get to know the grain of the green. The arrows show the direction in which the ball will break.

Identifying the grain of the green

The grain of the green is an important thing to consider, especially if you find you are letting putts slip by the hole and they are just missing when you thought they would drop. The odds are that you are ignoring the grain of the green. Take a look at the green in the sun from one direction – does it look shiny with a light green tinge? If so, then you are looking down the grain. If it appears darker, then you are looking against the grain. The grain will affect the break of the ball.

Putting with the grain

If you are putting with the grain of the green, expect the grass to help the ball on its way, thereby speeding up the putt. You do not need to hit the ball as hard, even if you are putting slightly uphill.

Putting against the grain

If the grass is slightly darker from you to the hole, you are putting against the grain, which will slow the putt down as the grass holds up the ball a touch.

Putting across the grain

Even if the putt appears to be flat, you could face break as the putt slows down if you are putting across the grain of the green. Make a check of the grain and adjust your line slightly – your ball will break with the grain.

Jargon buster

'Grain of the green' The direction in which the grass lies is known as the grain. All grass will lie in one direction, usually pointing towards the sun.

Putting on hills

Slopes and curves on greens are a pleasure and a curse. They look beautifully picturesque, and add character to the course, but can make the game incredibly difficult. If you are faced with putts straight up or straight down the hill, you can be forgiven for cursing your luck. Here are some hints for coping with slopes.

Practise pace perfection

Try this drill to gauge uphill and downhill putts. Head to a sloping putting green with three balls and two tees.

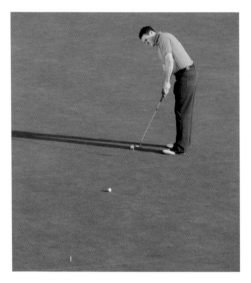

1 Place the tee pegs at either end of the slope, around 4.5 metres (15 ft) apart. Take your three balls to the higher tee-peg and putt down towards the lower tee. Try to learn from the reaction on the green and the pace of the roll.

2 Collect the balls and putt them back up the hill to the tee-peg at the top – the opposite putt to the one you have just made. Watch carefully and learn how each ball reacts to each pace of putt. Do this exercise a number of times and you will realize how downhill and uphill putts differ.

Putt beyond the hole

Always look to leave the ball beyond the hole. If you manage this, you will have given yourself a chance of letting the ball drop. A short putt will never go in, whereas a putt that runs a few metres past at least had a chance. 'Never up, never in' is an infuriating on-course cliché born from this common and annoying error.

Downhill putt trick

If you are faced with a slippery downhill putt, try this technique to adjust for the inevitable overhit. As you address the ball off the toe of the club, make your normal stroke, looking to make contact with the ball with that toe end. This part of the putter is more dead than the middle, so when it makes contact with the ball the transfer of energy is less efficient, leading to a softer strike. The result is that you will strike the ball gently, which is handy over a tricky downhill putt. Practise this trick shot before playing it in anger or the results could be disastrous.

The break on slopes

Putting uphill or downhill is tricky enough without throwing in a sideways slope. But you are unlikely to get a perfectly true uphill or downhill putt without some sideways slope, so knowing what the likely effect will be is important. Remember that when you are putting uphill gravity is knocking the energy out of the ball, taking speed and turn off it. So an uphill putt does not break as much as a flat putt and needs a firmer rap to get it up to the hole. Putting downhill with break is perhaps the most difficult problem you can face on the green. Gravity accelerates the ball down the hill adding energy and adding break, making it tough to control. Don't be too shy, though. about hitting the ball because break affects the ball more as it slows down.

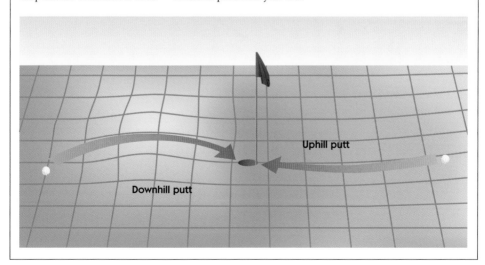

Uphill putt

Downhill putt

Pre-round pace preparation

Before you head to the first tee, apart from loosening up and getting all your golfing muscles firing, this is a great chance to come to terms with the greens. I have already explained how to build pre-round confidence over short putts; here are simple ways to help gauge the pace and fine-tune your touch before starting.

The stagger practice

Take around half a dozen balls onto the practice green – making sure they are the same make of ball you will use on the course – and find a quiet part of the green. Place all the balls on the ground in a straight line heading away from you. There is no need to have a specific target or hole for this drill. Address the first ball and putt it 4.5 metres (15 ft), then try to roll the next ball slightly beyond this first ball. Continue on down the line, rolling each ball just past the previously struck one. Your ultimate aim is to have a line of balls in a perfectly staggered formation, stretching across the green, finding a consistent feel for the putt and the green in the process.

Instant practice tip

For any drill where you are working on feel as part of your pre-round preparation and are developing a taste for the pace of the green, it is important to give yourself a number of different types of putt: uphill, downhill, left-to-right, right-to-left and so on. If you don't, you will be gauging one type of pace for the green, which will not fully equip you for the round ahead.

Keep your eyes on the hole

When you are on the practice green, trying to loosen your stroke and work on feel, place a ball on the green and go through your pre-shot routine, involving practice swings, while looking at the hole. This technique gives you direct visual information as you make the stroke, so it is a great way to gauge distance and work on feel. Keeping your eyes on the hole as you putt, address the ball, place the club behind it, look at the hole and leave your eyes there and then see how accurate you can be.

Change the distance of long putts

By the time you have finished this drill you will have a good feel for the pace of the putting surface over a variety of distances. Take your dozen balls and place them in a diagonal line, 1 metre (3 ft) apart and starting around 3 metres (10 ft) from the hole. Move to the ball nearest to the hole and try to sink it. It doesn't matter if you manage to or not; just try to make the putt roll beyond the hole at the very least. Now move to the ball behind that one, again trying to sink it, or leaving it beyond the hole. Continue in this way until you have putted all the balls.

Vary your targets

When you are practising, whether it is before a round or just general practice, try to vary your targets – sometimes putting to a hole, sometimes to a tee, sometimes to a towel laid on the ground or even to another ball.

Troubleshooting – pace problems

Two things are true about all golfers. Everyone has trouble at one time or another judging pace on the greens. Everyone has a natural in-built touch that is amazingly accurate – sometimes it is just difficult to realize and find that. So, if you are struggling to leave the ball dead from distance regularly, make these adjustments and release your inner touch.

The blind drill

1 When you are practising, give yourself a 4.5 metre (15 ft) putt. Stand over the ball and run through your routine and normal preparation, trying to find the pace of the putt. But before you play shut your eyes or pull your cap over your eyes and play the shot blind.

2 Try to judge the distance using all your other senses rather than sight. By cutting off one sense you intensify the others so they become much more effective, leading to a more instinctive and natural putting stroke.

3 When you have played the shot, guess where the ball finished and then take a look. See how wrong you were before playing the shot blind again. You will be amazed at how quickly your touch adjusts and how accurate you can be.

Improve your shot preparation

A common cause of bad touch and feel is poor shot preparation – an inconsistent routine. Work on your pre-shot routine in practice so it becomes second nature but add in some factors that may help. When you are reading the putt, picture in your mind's eye the ball rolling towards the hole and dropping.

As you take your practice strokes, keep this image clear in your mind and make sure the practice stroke you are

Make your pre-shot routine second nature.

making is the one you will use for real when you are over the putt. Take one final look at the hole, imagining the ball dropping just before you pull the trigger.

Roll with it

If you throw something to a friend, you never hurl it miles past the intended target. Yet this happens regularly on the golf course because golfers have not realized that natural ability.

To judge a long putt, stand behind the ball, looking at the hole, and imagine rolling it underarm close to the pin. Mimic an underarm throw, feeling the distance and pace. You need this feeling for the putt, so replicate it when you are over the ball.

How hard would you roll the ball at the hole?

Jargon buster

'Pulling the trigger' The moment in the golf swing or putting stroke when you first take the club back before striking.

Keep an image of the putt in your mind's eye.

Drills to improve your touch

Every golfer on the planet has an in-built ability and it just takes extra effort to discover and harness it. The practice green is a fantastic way to work on the artistic side of putting. Here are three simple drills that will make practice more fruitful and enjoyable.

Touch drill

1 Place six clubs in a line on the ground, so they are all parallel with 45 cm (18 inches) between each one. Take half a dozen balls and give yourself a putt 3 metres (10 ft) from the first club on the ground.

2 Now putt to the area of grass alongside the clubs. Try to make your first putt stop level with the end of the first club.

3 If you manage this, try to hold the second ball besides the second club. Carry on moving up the ladder with every successful putt. The trick comes when you fail to stop the ball the intended distance. If this happens, move back a level so you are putting to a club nearer. Continue until you complete it. Count how many strokes it takes you to finish and try to beat this next time you putt.

Impress touch in practice swing

One technique that will help your touch on the course enormously is to make practice swings while looking at the hole. Concentrate on feeling the length of the putt as you practise giving your technique direct messages from your eyes.

Add competition

Practice is always more profitable if you can add competition, especially if you are playing against another golfer. A good way to improve touch is to have a putting competition where you are putting to areas, as opposed to the hole, to work on your pace and touch.

Place three or four towels around the green at various points, flattened out to mark scoring areas, and take it in turns to putt three balls towards the towels, trying to stop each one dead on that scoring area. Use this scoring system: three points for a hit; one point if the ball runs through and stops within 1 metre (3 ft); minus one point if you are short.

The killer zone

This is a game you can play on your own. Any putt you hit will have the best chance of dropping if it is to stop in a 60 cm (2 ft) zone beyond the hole known as the killer zone. Pick a hole and place a club 0.6 metre (2 ft) beyond it and at right angles to you. Place another club 60 cm (2 ft) short, but not in the ball-to-target line, and a further club 1.2 metres (4 ft) short. All clubs should be parallel. Putt to the hole, trying to stop the ball in that killer zone 60 cm (2 ft) beyond the hole. Take 10 putts, scoring three points for holing out, two for finishing in the killer zone, zero for stopping 60 cm (2 ft) short and closer, minus one for being in that 1.2 metre (4 ft) zone and minus two for anything else.

-2
-1
0
2 The killer zone

Work on ball striking

If you are struggling for pace in practice, ignore the results of your putts and work purely on ball striking, feeling the ball come off the middle of the putter face. Your touch will return once you regain confidence in your ball striking.

The perfect pace for any putt

There is much debate about what is the perfect pace for any particular putt. Should the ball roll firmly at the hole, rapping the back before dropping, or is it best to nurse it forwards, letting the hole gather the ball as it loses pace and slips in over the front edge? Here are both sides of the argument.

The firm theory

Pros

• You are more likely to make the ball roll purely if you strike firmly.

• The harder you hit the putt, the less chance there is that the break will take hold and drag the ball off line.

If the ball rolls beyond the hole, it has a chance of dropping.

• The ball will always pass the hole, giving it a chance of dropping.

• You can see the break on your return putt as the ball passes.

Cons

• You may lose control of the putt and face a longer putt back.

• The ball has to hit the centre of the hole otherwise it will spin out.

The perfect-pace theory

Pros

• As the ball drops in at the perfect pace, you only have to hit a section of the hole and it will drop.

• You will almost certainly leave yourself a short return putt.

• The ball will tend to die towards the hole as it slows, as long as you have made an accurate read.

Cons

• You could easily leave the putt short, giving the putt no chance.

• The break will take more effect so you must have an accurate read.

It is all about the pace

If you are able to be specific with your putting touch, there is an answer to this conundrum, at least over a flat putt. Scientific research has discovered that there is an optimum pace for a putt that gives it the best chance of dropping. If you roll your putt with the aim of it stopping 45–60 cm (18–24 inches) past the hole, the ball will hold its line as it nears the hole, not taking any unexpected bumps and breaks, and will finish beyond the hole, giving it an excellent chance of dropping.

This is the science behind the theory, but in practice there are very few people who have such mathematical control over distance. It is more sensible to think in generic, tangible degrees such as 'Aim just beyond the hole'.

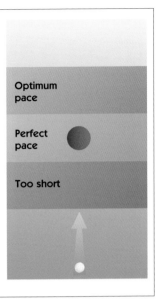

Uphill and downhill putting

When faced with a steep up- or downhill putt, the pace changes with the situation. For an uphill putt, try to knock the ball further past the hole than for a flat putt to ensure you make it to the hole. For a downhill putt, try to drop it in the front edge, cutting the risk of a 1 metre (3 ft) putt back.

For short putts take dead aim

If you are in any doubt whatsoever over the line of a short putt, aim straight at the middle of the hole and strike firmly. The positive stroke takes the break out of the putt.

Drop the ball in the front edge for downhill putts.

How weather conditions affect pace

One thing that golfers rarely take into account on the greens is the effect of the weather. The temperature, the amount of water in the air and the wind can lead to poor judgement of pace. Here are the most typical effects and difficulties you may encounter on the golf course.

Hot weather

If you are playing on a scorching day, the likelihood is that the grass on the greens will be short and parched, which in itself leads to quicker putting surfaces. Your ball is also more elastic and zippy. You will be smashing it further from the tee, hitting your irons longer than usual and also finding your putts roll faster. The flip-side to this is that if you are in an arid country the greens may be heavily watered, which can lead to slow-running greens.

Cold weather

Naturally, the effects are opposite to when it is hot. The grass on the greens may be slightly longer, which leads to slower running. Also, your ball and putterface will be much colder and so less elastic. This produces a less energetic strike, so you need to hit the ball firmly to make it roll far. An added problem is the touch in your fingers and muscles, which can become stiff in cold weather, leading to poor feel.

Watch the weather

There is rarely an even temperature and a perfectly calm, dry day on the golf course. Watching the weather is an integral part of any round of golf.

Sunny, hot weather will lead to quick, slick greens.

The effect of the wind

Although many golfers do not believe it, the wind can have as much effect on the ball when it is on the putting green as it can when you hit a driver. If you are playing on an especially windy day or on an exposed course such as a links in Scotland or Ireland, pay careful attention to the direction of the wind when you are putting.

If you are putting directly into a strong breeze, you will have to give the ball a firm rap. Wind can also negate the effect of any break you've seen on the putt. The opposite is true if you are putting with the breeze. You may suddenly find the ball accelerating away from you and taking extra break as a consequence of the wind.

Playing in the wet

● Wet greens will hold the ball up. Surface water immediately puts the brakes on any putt.

● If you are playing in the rain, unseen surface water can stop the ball dead in its tracks, so be wary.

● Be cautious when playing early in the morning as dew may affect your ball early in the round. It will also be gone later in the day, so the pace of the greens will change.

Wintry greens are always going to be slow and sluggish.

Reading greens

Reading greens is a tricky part of the game. Deciphering slopes and gradients is all part of the joy and frustration of this sport. Many golfers are unsure of what to look for, or how to look for it, when trying to read a putt. There are a few simple guidelines you can follow to make you a good green reader and to help discover the solutions to their mysteries.

Read as you approach

The biggest clues to how your putt will break are often easier to spot from a distance than when standing on the green. When you approach a green, don't daydream and chat to your opponent but have a look at where your ball has finished and glean a general overview of the lie of the land. Does the green slope hugely from front to back? Are there any dips and hollows that are visible from a distance? Reading from distance is surprisingly accurate and saves time on the green.

Read the putt as you approach the green to save time.

The water-jug trick

The late Payne Stewart had a clever way of deciphering break. He would stand behind his ball and imagine he had a large jug of water. He'd then tip it over in his mind and picture where the water would run – this would be the break of the putt.

Find the clues and use them

Any green has a number of clues that will give you an idea of the break. It is just a question of knowing where to look.

Pay attention to the general sculpture of the green. Where is it situated? If the architects have carved it out of a steep slope, then it is likely to break down this slope. Even if it appears flat when you are standing on it, this is just an optical illusion.

Take a look at the big features around you. Are you playing a lakeside hole? Are there mountains in the distance? It may seem strange but balls tend to break towards water and away from mountains in the distance. This does make sense when you think that water must flow from mountains to the lake and so must your ball.

Pay attention to your opponent's ball, even if they are not putting on your line. Any putt will give a clue to how the green lies near the hole and will provide a general impression of your own putt.

Look for the different clues on the green to improve your game.

Don't doubt yourself

When you are over your putt and about to pull the trigger, the read can often look different to the one you decided on. Stick with your original thought. Don't change at the last minute as this will lead to a hesitant, weak stroke.

Common problems and easy fixes

When you are faced with a long, curling putt, it is fine to make a good read but it is another thing to be able to play the ball down this line, actually making use of your read. One of the most common difficulties with reading greens is acting upon your insight and consequently putting accurately.

Can't see the read

Sometimes the green wins and the putting surface is a confusing mass of breaks, double breaks and flatness. However long you try, you know you'll struggle to figure this one out.

Cure:
work on pace alone

The pace of a putt actually determines a true read. A putt hit softly will take more break than a putt struck firmly. So, if you are ever in doubt over a putt, concentrate on the pace more than the line. If you roll the ball at a correct pace, the break may take the ball away from the hole, but you will never finish a great distance away, and you will also see how the green lies.

Tiger Woods believes the most important aspect of putting is ball-to-cup speed. He looks to hit putts so they never finish more than 30 cm (1 ft) beyond the hole. You cannot read a putt unless you have worked out the speed because pace determines line.

Jargon buster

'The apex of the putt' The point where the break of the green takes hold as the ball loses speed in the putt. It is the turning point of any particular putt.

Not making best use of your read

If you have made a read but the ball has not gone in the direction you intended, you have probably over-complicated the process of applying reading to putting. You need to break it down more simply.

Cure:
play to the apex
of the putt

Remember, you can only hit the ball once. All you can do is start the ball rolling on a straight line, so for that reason you need to pick one point and play to this. To keep the putt really simple, work out where you think the apex of the putt is, where the break of the putt will take hold, and putt directly at this by aligning your body and putterface to this one specific point.

The pace of your putt dictates the exact nature of this point, so if you intend to strike the ball firmly remember to choose a less acute angle.

Soft ← → Firm

Miss on the low side

Over longer distances, professionals always give the putt more 'room' than they initially think will be needed. If they miss the putt, they want to miss on the high side, so that the ball is always slowing down towards the hole. Sometimes they'll get lucky and one will drop.

Practice tips for reading putts

Reading the 'borrow' is down to practice. You have to hit enough putts to develop a sixth sense, where you can instinctively feel for the pace and line of a putt, bearing in mind that pace dictates the line. Here are some guides to practice drills and techniques that will help you hone that natural feel.

Line up your logo

There are markings on most putters and balls that help you strike the putt on your chosen line. Once you have picked the point you want to putt towards, line up the logo on the ball with this line. When you address the ball, try to align the marks on the back of the putterhead with the logo and ensure that your putterface is accurately aimed.

Hit to a tee-peg

Give yourself a curling 6 metre (20 ft) putt on the putting green. Read the putt and establish where the apex is, where you think your ball will turn towards the hole. Stick a tee-peg in here and hit a dozen putts towards the tee-peg. How accurate was your read? How did differently paced putts react to the break? This is a simple and easy way to learn about putting to an apex.

The big break

You will gain confidence in your ability to read putts as well as building a clear mental picture of how much a putt actually breaks in any particular situation with this practice. Try taking nine balls to the putting green and finding a good slope where you can line your balls up in a smooth, even arc along this slope. As you step to the ball nearest the hole, run through your pre-shot routine, reading the putt as normal, and try to hole out. Move to the next ball down the line and repeat the process until you have tried to hole each putt in turn.

Throw balls in the air

You may have realized that each putt you face on the course is different. You rarely have a straight putt and you rarely have

the same type of putt consecutively. Practising the same putt repeatedly is not simply realistic preparation. So, to add variety in your routine, take half a dozen balls to a quiet part of a green and throw them all in the air. Let them land and scatter naturally

around the green. They will end in a variety of positions around the hole, at different distances and on different lines. Move around each ball and, before trying to sink them, run through your pre-shot routine and read the putt carefully.

Watch ball past hole

When you run a putt past the hole, don't roll your eyes in frustration but watch how the ball breaks after the hole – this is your putt back and you are getting an instant read.

Techniques for reading greens

There are many weird and wonderful ways of analysing the borrow. You will see that each professional has a different approach; they are doing what they find has worked for them over the years. Here is a variety of different techniques used by golfers for deciphering slopes. Pick whichever works for you and implant it in your pre-putt routine.

The plumb line

This is the famous image of a golfer dangling their putter in front of their face and closing one eye. There is much debate as to whether this technique works or not, but many golfers feel it gives them a perspective they find useful. Hold the club in

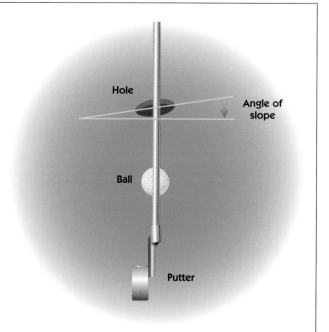

front of your face, closing one eye, so the club appears to dangle through the ball and the flag. If the flag appears to lean to one side of the putter shaft, this is the direction in which the ball will break. The bigger the lean, the greater the borrow.

Lying on the ground

A number of golfers find it helpful to get a worm's eye view of a putt by moving to the fringe of the green and lying so low that they can see the profile of the putting surface as accurately as possible. This can become a very time-consuming exercise but could be useful if you are struggling over a read or need to double-check your instincts.

Read putts from all angles

To get a very accurate read of a putt, look at the green from a number of different angles. Different perspectives can add a great deal of information as well as demystifying what can be a muddling situation. Always start your read from beyond the hole, so you are looking back at the ball.

Move on now so that you are between the ball and the hole, paying particular attention to the last third of the putt, the area where the ball will be dying in pace and the break will take the most effect.

Make a final check of your read by standing behind the ball. It is vital to make this angle your last, so you are able to visualize the ball rolling into the hole, along the break you have chosen.

Putt with instinct

Justin Rose, one of Europe's leading golfers, found he was over-analysing putts, which led to confusion and a suffocation of his natural flair and instinct. He ripped up his pre-shot routine and tried to let everything become more natural, artistic and less scientific – with great success. If reading putts becomes a detriment rather than an asset, only make a cursory glance at the break and then let your instinct take over.

Go with your first idea
If you ever doubt your read, stick with your first impressions – more often than not these are accurate, so trust your inner self to get it right the first time.

Reading different greens

An uphill putt with a 3 metre (10 ft) break from left to right on a parkland course will require a very different putt from a similar situation on a links course. Reading greens does vary between the different types of courses and the different weather conditions, so make sure you become flexible with your touch.

You will never conquer the greens if you are unable to read them.

Reading the break on quick greens

Quick greens will break more than a slower surface. Not only do you have to be careful with your stroke to avoid overhitting, but the borrows will also become accentuated, dragging the ball further from the target.

Reading the break on slow greens

Similarly, slower greens will not break as much. Parkland courses will typically have slower and flatter greens with the emphasis being on accurate iron-play and driving, as opposed to links courses, where good putting and the short game are at a premium.

The Stimp metre

The Stimp metre measures whether a green is quick or slow. It is a metal bar 1 metre (3 ft) long, with a groove on one side. A ball rests in that groove and the bar is slowly lifted at one end. The ball will eventually roll down the bar and across the green. The distance it rolls is its Stimp reading – a quick green is 3.6 metres (12 ft), an average green is around 2.7 metres (9 ft).

Reading greens

- Look for clues as you approach the green.

- Balls break away from mountains and towards areas of water.

- If in doubt, concentrate on pace more than on a complicated read.

- Aim for the apex of the break.

- Quick greens break more and slow greens break less.

Keep your ball as dry and clean as possible even in bad conditions.

Other factors that affect borrow

Wet weather will slow greens down so that the break is less accentuated. You can often use marks left in dew or moisture to gauge the amount the greens are breaking. Use the poor conditions to your advantage.

Greens that are bare due to lack of moisture or poor upkeep will have more borrow than lush putting surfaces. The lack of grass speeds the greens up, increasing the effect of the slope.

The grain of the grass will push the ball in its direction. If you are playing on a relatively flat surface, the ball is unlikely to swing against the grain.

DIFFICULT CONDITIONS

Coping with the wind

Wind on the golf course is commonplace. It adds to the richness of the sport, creates variety and renews the challenge of a familiar layout. It also makes life tough. Not only does wind buffet your ball from one side of the fairway to the other, it also bashes your body and swing around the course. Unless you are well prepared, wind will cost you matches.

When you are playing in the wind, make a firm base at address.

Stay relaxed and loose over the ball.

Key concern in the wind

The first things to worry about when putting in the wind are your posture and your address position. These are basics that should be good in any case, and the more solid your posture at address the easier putting in the wind becomes. The key is to stay stable and steady despite the stiff breeze – such steadiness comes from decent posture and a good address position.

Technique alteration

One simple way of improving balance and stability in the wind is to widen your stance. Grip down the putter slightly, as your centre of gravity will become lower, and will create a solid base with your feet more than a shoulders-width apart.

Maintain tempo and rhythm

Once you have this solid base, you need to make a solid stroke, which comes down to keeping your rhythm and tempo even. The great American golfer Johnny Miller won the Open Championship at Royal Birkdale in 1976 by maintaining his rhythm on the greens despite tough conditions and fierce competition. He did it by drawing a red dot with his wife's lipstick on the base of the grip. He concentrated on keeping the pace of that red dot even throughout the stroke. He did not even look at the ball, just kept his mind on that dot and so maintained his tempo.

Concentrate on the base of your club rather than the ball to maintain a consistent rhythm.

TOP TIP

Occasionally, the wind will be so strong it blows the ball as it sits on the green. If you have addressed the ball, grounded your club and it moves, you suffer a one-stroke penalty. If you don't ground your club, you can wait until the ball is still and play from where it lies. If in doubt, hover your putter and avoid penalty.

Be single-minded

When under pressure from the elements, it is vital to keep your mind clear with simple thoughts. Have one thought on which you concentrate throughout. Here is a selection of useful ideas you can fall back on when your technique is being blown across the course.

• Think of driving a drawing pin into the back of the ball with your putterhead.

• Concentrate on your follow-through and ignore the rest of your stroke.

• Look at the hole and become solely target-orientated, ignoring technique.

• Stay balanced, think balance and concentrate on this alone.

Think of driving a drawing pin into the ball.

Coping with match pressure

The most pressurized situations on golf courses are on the greens. This is the business end of the game, where matches are ultimately won or lost. Okay, the first tee is a nerve-wracking situation, but once it has gone it has gone. You have to putt on every hole and you have the chance to make good play count or lose your advantage with simple dropped shots. Coping with this pressure is a skill in its own right.

Simple pressure keys

When you feel the heat, your heart rate accelerates and your muscles tense. Both these changing factors lead to a jerky rhythm on the greens.

First, as you are walking to the green, take some long, deep breaths, exhaling slowly, in order to slow your heart rate down. The increased oxygen to your head will ease any tension.

Second, make a conscious effort to lighten your grip. Your hands express the nervousness in your body most explicitly and you can find yourself throttling the putter. By consciously easing off with your grip, you release the tension in your arms and can make a more relaxed stroke.

Make a conscious effort to loosen your grip under pressure.

Routine time

An important element in dealing with match pressure is to stick to your routine – the familiar, comforting cocoon that gives you confidence. Prepare for the pressure putt in exactly the same way as you would prepare for a simple 3 metre (10 ft) putt on the first hole. You must take the same time over each putt, whether it is your first putt in the round or a 1.8 metre (6 ft) putt to halve the match.

Crank up the pressure in practice

Pressure is always something you will feel on the course, so it is something that needs practice. You practise every other element of the game, so replicating pressurized situations is essential in making it through the heat unscathed. Try this pressure drill.

1 Place half a dozen balls around the hole in a perfect circle about 1 metre (3 ft) out. Move round the circle, holing each putt in turn. If you miss any, take all the balls out of the hole and start again. Keep going until you have sunk every putt.

2 Now move the balls back to 1.5 metres (5 ft) from the hole and repeat the process, starting again if you miss. Once you have successfully completed this, return to the 1 metre (3 ft) putts. Look to hole three sets from each distance and do not stop until you manage it.

TOP TIP

Never forget that, whatever the situation, you are completely in control. Nothing your opponent can do will affect how you strike your ball. For this reason, you must first think to play each shot individually, then think to play against the golf course and finally think to play against your opponent. Reversing this order will lead to disaster as you worry about elements beyond your control.

Different types of greens and grass

One of the joys of golf is the infinite variety of locations and types of course. This leads to endless arguments about which type of course is best, which is the sternest test, which is the purest challenge. Each type of course has different characteristics, using differing grass, especially around the green. Putting on a links is nothing like putting on a parkland course.

A links green

Links courses tend to be larger than parkland courses and, especially at the height of summer, not so clearly defined. The short, tight fairways run seamlessly and smoothly into the putting surface. You can happily find yourself playing a 24 metre (80 ft) putt across a mountainous landscape – it is all part of the joy and beauty of a links course.

The tighter, shorter nature of the grass does make links courses more slick than parkland (although this is not always the case). The speed of the greens exaggerates the break, making putting a more challenging prospect.

Parkland courses are tree-lined with water hazards.

Variety is the spice of life

To improve an all-round game, it is essential to play a variety of courses, as they demand such different skills. Golfers who do not travel tend to suffer – especially at the highest level. The best golfers in the world put in the air miles – Ernie Els and Tiger Woods play across the globe with great success – and their counterparts who prefer to remain around home comforts lack the versatility in their games that this variety brings.

Parkland courses

Typically, parkland greens are slower and softer than links. There is a strong definition between the fringe and the green, and approach shots need to be high, spinning and accurate. Often, parkland greens will be smaller than on links, so the slopes are less brutal. That said, many of the newer parkland layouts have produced vast greens with a variety of tiers that require careful approach play. To help your putting, you need to hit as close to the pin as possible at all times. On parkland courses especially, use a course map for accurate distances. Make sure you know where the map measures the reading from – the back, middle or front of the green. There can be as much as a three-club difference.

Putting on a slower green

1 Address the ball as normal, with a balanced and stable posture. Keep a simple, pendulum back-and-through stroke, keeping your wrists still and steady. When playing on softer greens, however, it can be useful to have a small amount of 'release' in your putting stroke.

2 As you take the club back, don't be afraid to let your wrists break very slightly with the weight of the club. Don't overdo it; simply allow a small kink and flex on your backswing.

3 On the throughswing, again let your wrists break with the weight of the putterhead. This is the release. By allowing your wrists this flexibility, you encourage a slight 'hit' in the stroke that can help the ball roll smoothly across slower surfaces.

Putting at different times of day and year

Golf is unusual as a sport in that it is played all day long (light permitting) and all year round. Playing at different times affects your ball in different ways from tee to green (the ball flies further in summer). It also has a crucial effect on the putting greens, which is often ignored.

Greens change as the day goes on.

Playing in the morning

• Greens will be shorter and running quicker if freshly mown.

• Watch out for any dew just below the surface as this can slow the roll of your ball.

• The direction of the grass cut dictates the direction of the grain.

Playing in the afternoon or evening

• The grass has had all day to grow and may well run slower than earlier.

• The grass may have time to dry out and be slightly crusty, running quicker than earlier.

• More golfers will have walked on the greens, so they will have more spikemarks and pitchmarks – you can repair pitchmarks but not spikemarks.

Greens change – look at the scores

Follow the first few rounds of a US or European Tour event, where the field is so large they have morning and afternoon starts; notice a pattern in the scores, depending on how the greens have changed through the day. When greens are tough in the morning, scores will be higher than when they've eased up later on and vice versa.

Putting in winter

Playing golf in the winter, even if you do live in a sunny climate, is different from summer golf. As the sun does not rise so high in the sky, the greens do not dry out as quickly so they remain slower. In addition, greenkeepers will not cut the greens as short or as frequently as they might during the height of summer.

This all adds up to the greens becoming slower and for this reason taking less break. Even with shorter putts, the borrow on greens is less severe than on a summer's day.

Winter golf is almost a different sport to the summer game.

Different types of grass

Bermuda grass: this entangling, thick-set grass may make it hard for you to swing your club through it.

Rye grass: if you are playing on rye grass, the ball will break less on the putting green.

Bent grass: this type of grass breaks the least, so check with the pro before you head out.

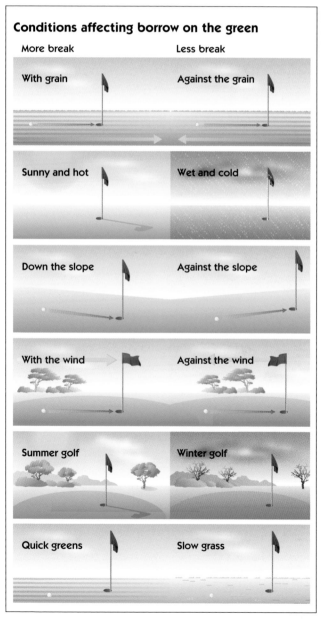

Conditions affecting borrow on the green

More break	Less break
With grain	Against the grain
Sunny and hot	Wet and cold
Down the slope	Against the slope
With the wind	Against the wind
Summer golf	Winter golf
Quick greens	Slow grass

TROUBLESHOOTING

When you feel your putting is not firing on all cylinders, head onto the course and make a note of where you are going wrong. Are you consistently missing putts to one side of the hole, or are you leaving them all short, or even overhitting? I guarantee that a pattern will emerge. This section will iron out consistent problems and help you regain your form.

Always hitting putts to the right

If you find your putts are sliding down the right side of the hole, despite a good feeling off the putterface, you could be doing a number of things wrongly. Most commonly, the problem is one of two things – poor alignment or poor stroke path (see opposite). It is always worth making a check on both before deciding on the best way to cure your problem.

Cure: better alignment

1 You may often be aligning your body accurately but with your shoulders right of the target line, forcing you to swing your shoulders down, hitting right. So place the club behind the ball with your right hand only.

2 Next, bring your left hand onto the grip. This will make the alignment of the shoulders natural and accurate. Add this set-up drill into your standard pre-shot routine.

3 Finally, concentrate on swinging the putter down your shoulder line and directly at the target. As your feet and knees were already parallel, the putt will be accurate as long as your stroke path remains on that target line.

Poor stroke path

Most golfers try to swing the putter straight back and straight through, like a pendulum. Swinging the club slightly inside the line is a fine technique also – the swinging-door method – but you may find yourself in trouble if you take the club too far on the inside.

Such a position will lead to problems at impact. If you take the putter too far behind you, you will struggle to bring it back square at impact, which means the clubface will aim right as it makes contact with the ball. This will lead to a block, however good your initial aim and read of the putt.

Cure: improving stroke path

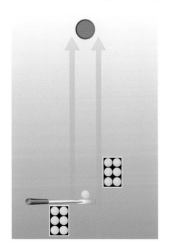

1 To keep your swing path in check, find a flat part of the green and take a 3 metre (10 ft) putt to a hole or to a tee in the ground. Place a box of balls inside the line behind your putter. Place another box outside the line and beyond the ball.

2 Now make the putt but avoid hitting either of the barriers in place. As you take the club back, if you touch the box of balls inside the line, your club will be swinging off line and you may well block.

3 As you swing through, look to keep the putterhead swinging comfortably towards the target and not hitting that box in front of your ball. Practise until missing the boxes becomes second nature and you'll not block again.

Always hitting putts to the left

Hitting putts left regularly can originate from similar problems to putts blocked right, but through opposite causes. Often, excess hand action in the stroke will drag the putt left, as a result of tension or through looking to see where the putt will finish. Here are two simple solutions to iron out pulled putts.

Jargon buster

'Pulled putts'

When a putt misses to the left of the hole; again as a result of faulty technique.

Cure: better alignment

1 Again, good body alignment mixed with poor shoulder lines can cause difficulties. If your body aims parallel to the target line, but your shoulders align left, you will pull the putt. First, place the club behind the ball and place your right hand on the grip.

2 Now bring your left hand onto the grip. You will naturally align yourself accurately as it will feel uncomfortable to aim your shoulders left of the target. It is vital that the putterface aims directly at your target, or this drill will not help.

3 Now concentrate on taking the putterhead back along the target line. Again, if you think to swing along your shoulders, then this will happen naturally and you will make an accurate roll towards the hole. Adding this set-up into your standard pre-shot routine will help deal with on-course difficulties.

Poor stroke path

Swinging the club straight back and straight through is the aim. A common problem is golfers taking the club outside the line as they swing. The putterhead moves further away from them in the first movements of the stroke, as opposed to inside and behind.

As the putter is outside the line, the golfer has to bring it back to the ball cutting across the ball-to-target line, so the putter ends swinging to the left of the hole, unsurprisingly taking the ball along with it. The result is an ugly pull and putt missed left.

Cure: the flag drill

One remedy for poor stroke path can be tried on a quiet flat green, giving yourself a 3 metre (10 ft) putt and using the flag. Taking the pin from the hole and standing behind the ball, lie the flag on the ground close to but outside your ball and parallel to the ball-to-target line.

With the flag in place, hit a number of putts aiming to swing the club along the line of the pin on the ground. If you strike the pin with the putterhead on your backswing, you will cut across the target line and pull the putt.

Keep your club swinging towards the hole, using the pin as a guide. The distance between your putterhead and the pin should not change on your back- or throughswing. Practise until this is consistent.

Always leaving putts short

If you find that you are leaving many putts short, then you are committing golf's worst sin. Never getting the ball up to the hole is a serious problem for a number of reasons.

• It is a negative way to miss the putt – you never gave it a chance. If it had run just past the hole, it could also have dropped.

• Your read of the putt is redundant – the ball takes more break as it loses speed so you could never have judged the borrow accurately.

• Hesitancy will creep into the rest of your game.

Ignore the hole

One clever way to make sure your ball rolls to the hole and beyond is to ignore it. Walk behind the hole, find a point 1 metre (3 ft) beyond the cup – a mark in the grass, a leaf or a piece of dirt – and when lining up your putt use this as your focus point. If you strike a good putt, the ball will roll just beyond the hole at optimum pace; if not, the ball will still reach the hole.

Check your equipment

If you are leaving a number of putts short, it may be worth looking at your putter. Contrary to what your instincts tell you, a putter with less weight behind it – a blade or heel-toe putter – will help you strike the ball more firmly than a heavy mallethead. The lighter club makes your stroke more aggressive due to the lack of weight and an intuitive need to hit firmly. If you are coming up short, find a light club.

Hole

Improve your ball striking

Leaving putts short regularly can often be down to poor ball striking. If the ball is not coming off the middle of the club, you will not be transferring all your energy into the ball and it is likely to finish short. Try this drill to help.

1 Take three pillows onto a flat surface. Place two side by side so they have a hole's width between them. Place the third behind these two, so it is in line with the gap.

2 Take your putter and tape two tees to the face and either side of the middle of the club so that they are a ball's width apart. Make sure that the tees frame the hitting area on the club.

3 With your adjusted putter, strike balls through the gap in the pillows. If you make an off-centre strike, the ball will squirt right or left, but the pillows will stop it.

4 When you strike the ball off the middle, the ball will travel between the pillows and be stopped by the third. This means you can practise a variety of putts of different length anywhere without having to retrieve balls.

Picture the ball coming back

To help get the ball up to the hole, in your pre-shot preparation, instead of picturing the ball rolling towards the hole and into it, picture it coming in the opposite direction – rolling out of the hole and back to your putter. This will trick the mind into striking more positively because the desired outcome is the start of the thought process.

Overhitting putts regularly

Overhitting putts can become a real problem. Racing a putt past the hole and leaving yourself with a longer one back than you had originally is disheartening and embarrassing. This problem strikes sporadically during a round, so take heart that it is not a permanent problem and is usually a result of conditions.

Instant tips to rein in a hot putter

● Grip the club more lightly with your bottom hand. A heavy grip leads to a heavy stroke, so by loosening your grip, especially the bottom hand which drives added power through the ball, you will regain touch.

● Use a heavier putter and you will find that you instinctively stroke the ball more gently.

● Try shortening your backswing. The length of the backswing will determine the power in the putt.

● Concentrate on maintaining tempo while shortening the distance you take the putter back.

● In dire emergencies, look to start the ball off the toe of the club. Address the ball opposite the end of the club and look to use this part of the putterface to strike the ball. This softens the strike and leads to a gentler roll.

Pro-Am chaos

Overhitting putts is a common affliction for amateurs playing in Pro-Ams, especially the Pro-Ams that precede Tour events. The greens for these tournaments are far quicker than amateur greens, so if you are lucky enough to play in a Pro-Am, you need to become a gentle putter.

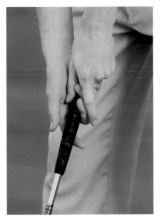

Hold your putter lightly with your bottom hand.

Shorten your backswing but maintain tempo.

Using the toe end of your putter can deaden the strike and soften a heavy-handed touch.

Rediscover your range

When you are struggling with pace on the greens, the worst thing you can do is hope it will get better. Here is a simple and effective practice, particularly if you are overhitting putts.

By putting a variety of distances alternately, you will quickly retune your touch. Start by taking four balls to the putting green and hit one putt around 9 metres (30 ft) to no particular target, concentrating on the ball strike. With your next ball, look to putt half that distance – only 4.5 metres (15 ft). Aim to hit the third ball about half the distance again, then finally you should try to stop the final ball only 1 metre (3 ft) from the spot from which you are putting.

Keep a record of how accurate you are by giving yourself points and try to beat your best score whenever you carry out this practice.

Jargon buster

'Pro-Am' A tournament, often played the day before a professional event, where amateurs compete in teams with one professional; usually played as a stroke-play event off full handicap.

Putting long – not all bad

Out of all the afflictions you can suffer on the putting greens, this is perhaps the best. Over-hitting putts is a positive way to miss, if such a thing is possible. At least you have given the ball a chance of dropping by hitting it beyond the hole. The ball may hit the hole, pop up and drop in. You will also see how your putt back will break by watching the ball as it passes the hole.

Long-term 'yips' recovery

I touched on the yips previously (see page 44), but it is a condition that needs closer attention. Many great golfers have become ordinary players because of this painful problem. Cures are never easy and never appear overnight – they require practice, training and careful preparation. Here are a few suggestions and thoughts that might help.

The armpit drill

1 It doesn't sound nice, I agree, but it may well help. Head to the practice green, place a club under your armpits so that it runs along your chest. Take your address position and knock in those 0.6 metres (2 ft), 1 metre (3 ft) and 1.2 metre (4 ft) putts that have given you trouble.

2 The club across your shoulders makes you feel the connection between your arms and your shoulders acutely. It acts as a chain, holding them in place. This concentrates the mind on the correct stroke – a rocking motion from the shoulders and not a flick from the wrists.

Change the putter

Many golfers have found relief from the yips by changing their putters and playing with a longer club – either a broomhandle or a belly putter. Once you have overcome the embarrassment of your playing partners' sniggers, this is an effective method of overcoming the yips. The broom essentially makes you putt one-handed, so there is no conflict between left and right hand – one cause of the yips. A belly putter anchors the club in your midriff so your hands act just as a guide.

Expert's eye on yips

The yips are the cause of much ongoing research and debate in various academic institutions across the world. A multitude of theories abound and a multitude of attempted cures work and fail in equal measure. There are a number of constants, though, and one is the idea that the yips sufferers tend to be the analysers, the golfers who pay too much attention to their hands, their putter, their shoulders, anything in fact, except the ultimate goal – hitting a ball in a hole.

Golf psychologist and guru to the stars Dr Bob Rotella writes, 'Players who develop the yips tend to be players who don't understand that good putting is an uncontrolled, subconscious act.'

Ongoing research is looking into the cause and cure of the yips.

Sam Snead on the yips

'I've gotten rid of the yips four times but they hang in there. You know those 0.6 metre (2 ft) downhill putts with a break? I'd rather see a rattlesnake.'

The most effective solution

It is a struggle but the only way to overcome the yips permanently is to dismantle your putting and start again with a breezy attitude. Look to enjoy putting again. Accept the misses, then forget them and remember, instead, each time you do hole out. Try to laugh away any difficulties. Crucially, try to avoid thinking of the mechanics of putting and concentrate on the ball rolling into the hole.

To help, when you face a short putt on the course, run through your pre-shot routine as normal, address the ball, take one last look at the hole, then shut your eyes. Now putt. By taking the visual reminder away from what you are doing, you are more likely to stay relaxed.

Putting with your eyes shut can help with the yips.

PUTTER EXTRA

Did you know that your putter doesn't have to be used on a green and that you can use it anywhere? Did you know that your putting technique is not the preserve of the short stick but that you can employ it in a variety of situations? The versatility of your putter and putting is unmatched in golf, so add extra weapons to your game by trying some of the shots on the following pages.

You are allowed to use your putter anywhere on the golf course.

Using your putter around the green, from the fringe or apron, is always a good option. Here's why:
• When you have no hazards to carry, there is no point in risking a chip shot that leaves the ground, leaving it open to the elements.
• A bad putt will always finish closer to the hole than a bad chip, whereas a good putt is just as good as a good chip.
• When you are playing from a bare lie, it is difficult to get a round-bottomed wedge to the bottom of the ball.
• The wind will affect a putt less than a chip, as it is kept at ground level.
• It is harder to fluff a putt than a chip, where thinning the ball and catching it heavy are relatively commonplace.

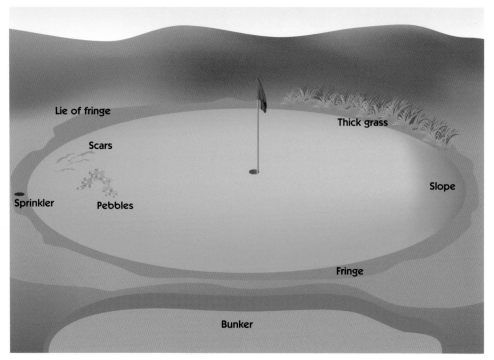

Labels on image:
- Lie of fringe
- Thick grass
- Scars
- Slope
- Sprinkler
- Pebbles
- Fringe
- Bunker

To putt or not to putt

This is often a question you will have to ask yourself around the greens. Here is a quick guide to the elements that you should take into account when faced with this awkward dilemma. Remember the basic principle, though; go with the shot that you know will leave you closer to the hole.

The ball's lie

The most crucial element is how the ball lies. If it sits down in a pocket of grass or a divot, it is probably best to use a wedge to get to the bottom of the ball.

Length of fringe

If the grass around the edge of the green is too long, a ball rolling through it could become ensnared, so pace is difficult to judge.

Slopes on the green

Are you putting directly on to a severe slope on the green? If so, it may be wiser to lob the ball to a flat and true part of the green.

Scars on the ground

Putting through divots, across paths and over sprinkler heads is haphazard and even dangerous. Ensure you have a clean route through to the flag.

Assess the green to determine whether you should putt at all.

Hazards

You cannot putt through bunkers, streams or hollows filled with deep grass. Sounds stupid, but it has been tried.

Putting on different types of course

You are more likely to use your putter from off the green when you are play-ing a parched links or heathland course than if you are playing a lush parkland course with well-defined greens, fairway and rough. So if you are heading to the seaside, practise your long putts.

Versatility of the putting technique

Not only is the putter a tool you can use in a variety of places around the course but the technique is also versatile, as long as you have the confidence and imagination to use it. A solid, reliable stroke can help you get up-and-down from a number of awkward lies.

The chip-putt

When you are faced with a short carry over thick grass before the putting surface, using the chip-putt technique will help. Take a 7- or 8-iron and address the ball as you would a putt, using a putting grip, posture and set-up but with the ball slightly more central in your stance.

Jargon buster

'Up-and-down' When a golfer holes out in two shots from off the green, usually when chipping. This often takes the form of a chip close to the hole followed by a short putt.

1 Chip the ball using a simple putting stroke. Take the club straight back, rocking your shoulders with little or no wrist action and play the shot as though it is an extended putt.

2 Accelerate through the ball as you would any putt, making sure you swing further through than back. The ball will pop up, fly the short distance over the entangling and thick lie, then roll onto the green. This shot is ideal for playing over 18 metres (60 ft) at the longest; any further and you need an orthodox chip.

The bellied wedge

Another situation where a putting technique can come in handy is in playing the bellied-wedge shot. If your ball nestles against the first and second cut of the fringe, it can be tricky to make a consistent strike into the back of the ball with an orthodox chip shot, using a short-iron.

1 Escape this awkward situation by using a wedge and 'thin' the ball on purpose – hit the centre of the ball with the leading edge of the clubface. There's no need to touch the grass.

2 Use your putting stroke so that the clubface moves low and straight through the target line at impact.

The 3-wood chip

If you are playing from entangling fringe grass, chipping cleanly becomes hazardous, with your clubhead liable to snag. By using a fairway wood, the larger head sweeps through the grass making a clean strike.

Practise perfection

All shots are fun when they work but disastrous when they go wrong. They are worth practising before releasing on the course in anger, to avoid any horror holes.

1 Take a putting grip and address the ball as though it is a putt. Then rock your shoulders back and through the line as you would with a normal putt.

2 The ball will pop out of the awkward position, landing on the putting surface firmly and rolling close. The ball will fly further than a usual chip, so play gently.

Versatility of the putter

The putter is not just for the greens. It is a weapon of mass importance in your short-game armoury and beyond. The putting technique is the most simple in the sport and the putter should be the easiest club in the bag to use consistently. That is why it can be a reliable option, even in the least promising situations. All you need is courage.

Use the toe end

If your ball finishes in thick fringe grass, it can be difficult to get a club to the back of the ball, even if you do opt to use a fairway wood (see page 103). If this is the case, take a look at your putter. Does it have a relatively thin head with a square toe end?

If the answer is yes, you can use that toe end to great effect. Address the ball as normal but turn the club so it is sideways – perpendicular to the ball-to-target line.

Now putt using the toe end to strike the ball. The advantage of this technique is that the club head can easily slice through the entangling grass without becoming snagged.

Toe-end practice drill

Putting with the toe end of the club on the practice green is a fantastic method of improving your ball striking as you must be accurate. Any off-centre strikes will shoot sideways. A 10-minute session working with this drill helps build your confidence and the ball's roll.

Bumping it in the air

If your ball has nestled down in a divot or a sucking lie in Bermuda rough, striking cleanly with control becomes a lottery. This is really a shot that you should only play after substantial practice but one way to overcome this lie is to use your putter to loft the ball out of the hole.

Loft and putter are not words that often go together, but if you strike down on the back of the ball, almost vertically, with your putterhead the ball will pop up and out of this tricky lie with topspin and will roll towards the hole. You need to find a balance between a downward and a forward blow that drives the ball down and up but also advances it.

Putting from the trees

Again, this may sound crazy, but if you find yourself in trees and need to chip back to the fairway don't forget your putter. As long as the ground is relatively bare – which it often is – a putter will not loft the ball in the air, bringing overhanging branches into play. It also requires only a short backswing – perfect for escaping.

Three golden questions to ask before using the putter in different places

If the answer to any of these is 'yes' then put it back in the bag.

- Is the lie too bad to merit the use of the putter?
- Does the ball have to carry any trouble?
- Is another type of shot more likely to finish closer?

Putting out of a bunker

Okay, this may sound crazy but using a putter from a bunker can be the sensible and safe shot to play. As long as you use the correct technique and select the right occasion on which to play the shot, you will find the ball finishes closer more often than if you used a high-risk wedge. So ignore the muffled surprise from opponents and playing partners and knock it dead.

Key rules for putting out of a bunker

- Make sure the lip of the bunker is smooth and shallow – you cannot putt over a severe lip.

- Check the ball sits on top of the sand and is not plugged.

- The texture of the sand must be hard – any soft, fluffy sand will gather like snow around the ball.

- Make sure there is a clear run to the green and you don't have to carry rough or heather before reaching the putting surface.

Playing the shot

1 To play this shot, address the ball as a normal putt but make two changes. Do not ground your club – you are in a hazard and you will suffer a two-shot penalty in strokeplay and you'll lose the hole in matchplay. Dig your feet into the sand.

2 Make a full and aggressive swing at the ball. You have to be positive with this shot otherwise it will not escape the trap.

3 Accelerate through the ball, trying to catch it as cleanly as possible without taking any sand at all. Use your normal putting technique with a long backswing.

Playing chip shots

Many golfers do not realize that playing chip shots on the green, although not encouraged, is perfectly legal. You are allowed to use any club you want on the green; there are no special provisions made for putters.

1 Play as a normal chip with the ball opposite your right foot and an open stance.

2 Make a long backswing to ensure your clubhead travels fast through the ball.

3 Accelerate the clubhead through impact – this is vital for catching the ball cleanly.

Why would I want to chip on a green?

There are a few occasions when chipping is better:

• When faced with an enormous putt; likely on links courses.

• If the green is sloping and you want to land on the flattest section.

• If an awkwardly shaped green means you have to putt through the fringe or rough to reach the hole.

What to look out for

Unsurprisingly, you are unlikely to be best friends with the greenkeeper if you make a regular habit of this. Try to take the ball as cleanly as possible – little or no divot is your aim – to preserve the putting surface, and try not to fly the ball too high, creating another pitchmark. Use a pitching-wedge, as this is not designed to slide under the ball like a sand-iron.

The seven out of ten rule

Whenever you are looking at an unorthodox shot, make sure it is the correct option by using the seven out of ten rule: would you complete the shot successfully seven times out of ten? If the answer is yes, then it is worth the risk. Otherwise, have a rethink and play percentage golf.

Indoor putting practice

If you are bored at home, the rain is whipping the windows, or you are in the middle of a long day in the office and need a bit of relaxation, you can put in a great deal of useful practice on your putting technique with a few simple and safe indoor drills.

Putt to a coffee mug

When you are enjoying some carpet-putting, it is best to have a target. A coffee mug laid on its side makes a fantastic hole. You have to be very precise to strike the ball so that it rolls into the centre of the cup; otherwise it will spin out sideways and not enter. The rim of the mug also adds an obstacle for the ball to roll over – this helps you to strike more positively and firmly through the ball because you know it cannot 'topple in'.

Knock over a marker

Take a marker pen and place it on its end. Give yourself a 1.8 metre (6 ft) putt across the carpet and aim to roll the ball so it just knocks over the marker pen. You don't want to knock it flying – but you need to strike it firmly enough to knock it over. You will also have to be dead-eyed, as a sideways blow will not topple the marker as easily. See how many times out of ten you can knock it over – try to complete a perfect set.

Have a disco

Here is a great way to improve touch and accuracy on the greens during your winter or weather breaks.

For this indoor practice, you can cut out three paper circles 10 cm (4 inches) in diameter and give each one a different score – 3, 1, –1 for example. When ready to play, you can place the discs in a line flat on the carpet, with the highest score in the middle and the lowest nearest to you. Giving yourself a 1.8 metre (6 ft) putt, try rolling the ball so that it stops on the highest scoring disc. If you miss the discs altogether, score –2. Add up your score over ten balls and then try to beat this.

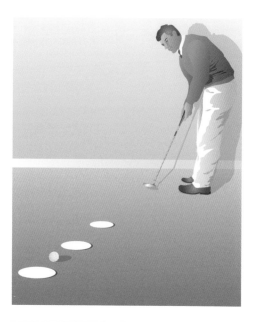

Bash the skirting board

This is a drill that works for alignment, aim and basic accuracy. Take the same discs that you've used for the disco drill and prop them up against the skirting board, with the highest-scoring disc in the centre. Give yourself a longer putt across the carpet – as long a putt as you are able to manufacture – and hit ten balls to build a score, again scoring –2 for a complete miss. You will soon start to build consistency in terms of alignment and accuracy by trying to better your scores.

Don't make it too different

It is tricky to run through your pre-shot routine when you are in a suit in the office and carpets don't tend to have huge breaks. But do make your putting as similar to the real thing as possible by using your actual putter and balls – not some novelty indoor set you may have been given for your birthday.

MIND GAMES AND TACTICS

Once you have become confident in your technique, the most prosperous way to move your game and especially your putting forward is through the power of the mind. Golf is a mental game – the stronger your thought processes, the better your scores. Golf is about eliminating self-doubt, playing with confidence and playing the right shots – once you have these under control, you are on your way to shooting serious numbers.

Keep even throughout

Just as the tempo of your stroke must remain even through the round, keep your inner tempo the same for 18 holes. Never become too disheartened when things go badly and, more importantly, do not get over-excited once you have sunk a huge putt or knocked in a birdie. Staying in control means dealing with highs and lows in a similar fashion.

Have a calming thought, a song, a peaceful mental image, a simple trigger that transports your mind to a relaxed, even area, one that is devoid of any on-course excitement.

Lose count of your scores

To help stay even throughout, ignore your scorecard. Just write the numbers down on each hole without keeping a running tally. This helps you concentrate on each individual putt at a time, irrespective of outside forces such as, 'I need this to go two under/keep my card going...'. The pressure you feel is all about the immediate situation and not the larger, more oppressive ideas. By ignoring your score, you will not get ahead of yourself and will focus solely on the job in hand.

Take pressure off by concentrating solely on the hole you are playing.

One key thought can help your technique stay sound under pressure.

Putt with instinct or analysis

What sort of person are you – a quick, hectic type or a laid-back, relaxed individual, or are you somewhere in between? Putt in a way that reflects your personality. If you live life in a carefree manner, putt with instinct. If you prefer control and order, be more analytical on the greens.

Practise pressure during practice rounds with games that penalize mistakes.

Empty your mind

Thinking about technique and working on technique is for the practice green and driving range. Trying new thoughts, grips and strokes while you are playing a match is dangerous and stupid. You need to concentrate on the game rather than think about how you are striking putts. To help maintain a balance between a solid technique and mental toughness, it is handy to have a simple swing thought – but only one. It may be 'grip gently' or 'take putter back slowly' – a simple, easy thought that will keep your technique on track while staying in the match.

Practise pressure

You need to prepare for pressure situations so you can cope with them on the course. If you are playing a practice round before a big game, take some money in note form on to the course with you. Every time you three-putt, leave a note at the bottom of the cup for the group behind. If you are not putting so well, this will hurt. If you are not prepared to risk a small fortune on your fragile technique, make a donation to charity as penance instead.

The key moments in any round

Any round of golf contains its crucial moments and important times. This may be down to match pressure but there are the same moments in any round that you have to deal with sensibly in order to overcome them. The first and last greens are vital for starting and finishing successfully. Bouncing back after a major or minor disappointment is also central.

Coping with the first green

We have all been there – you have hit a half-straight drive nervously from the first tee, have reached the green eventually, then suffered a three-putt to drop two shots. The only thing you can do to overcome first-green nerves and discover your touch before you start, is to warm up properly. A warm-up is not a practice.

You are not changing your stroke but rather reminding and warning your golfing muscles what is in store. Don't hit too many practice putts. Putt to tee-pegs and areas from distance as opposed to holes – it is not

Warm up by sinking short putts for confidence.

helpful to warm up through misses. Before you leave the green, sink ten short putts in succession to give your body positive feedback before you start.

Dealing with the last green

The big problem with the 18th green is the 'job done' syndrome. You have not finished your round until that final putt has dropped. Do not get ahead of yourself and drop one or two careless shots through negligence. Make a special effort to focus as you walk onto the green, running through your pre-putt routine as usual and only thinking about the bar when you have actually finished.

Only think about that post-match drink when you are post-match.

Don't be afraid to let frustration out discreetly.

Coping with disaster

The way in which golfers respond to disasters on the course is often the difference between high- and single-figure handicap players. By taking poor holes badly, you can disrupt the rest of your game. Follow a three-putt with a birdie, using this quick guide.

• Let it out. This does not mean smashing up course furniture and swearing at your opponents, but if you are seething with your own game it can be constructive to discreetly let out the anger. Make quick practice swings on the next tee, give yourself space from your opponents and silently scream into your cap. Obtaining an instant release, then going back to normal, is a human, constructive reaction to frustration.

• Forget it. This is easier to do once you have let that anger out. Focus on the next shot: there is nothing you can do about your misread or mishit on the last hole. Sink back into your pre-shot routine and look forward, not back.

• Think how good you are. Instead of rueing the missed chance or dropped shot, think of the long putts you have holed during the round and the shots you have put next to the pin.

Divide the round into mini-courses

A simple method of moving on after a poor hole is to divide the round into six mini-courses consisting of three holes each. Give yourself a par – one that would be a good but also a realistic score for you – for each set and play to it. If you are one or two over your par, ignore that score and concentrate on the next mini-course.

Aggressive practice swings can release annoyance.

Tactics on the green

Your tactics and shot selection around the course become more acutely important as you approach the green. There are a number of precautions and tactics you can employ to make the most of your situation, put your opponents under the greatest pressure and increase your chances of holing your putts.

Think about your approach

You should be thinking about your first putt as you are eyeing up your approach shot. Always look to leave yourself an uphill putt. Uphill putts are much easier to control than downhill ones; they do not break as much and will not take the ball away from the hole once it passes. Instead of smashing the ball as close to the flag as possible, look at the slopes on the green and keep your ball below the hole.

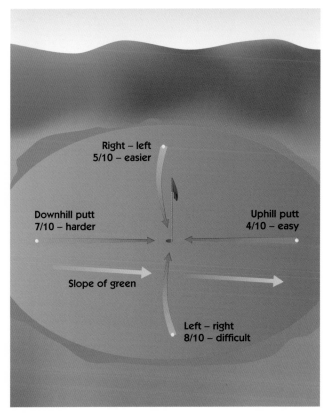

Right – left
5/10 – easier

Downhill putt
7/10 – harder

Uphill putt
4/10 – easy

Slope of green

Left – right
8/10 – difficult

Assess the slope of the green to plan how to control your putts.

Right to left

For right-handed golfers, playing a left-to-right putt is always more tricky than a right-to-left. There is no science behind this statement but ask any experienced golfer which shape of putt they'd prefer and the answer would be unanimous. The reason? If the ball is sliding away from your body, you feel less in control of the shot and alter your stroke, causing missed putts. If you have the ability with your approach shots, always look to give yourself a right-to-left putt if you are right-handed.

Use the opposition

You must always make use of your opposition when you are on the green. Pay attention to where their ball has finished; note how it reacted as it hit the putting surface. Where did it break? How did it roll? As your opponent putts, you are not allowed to stand directly behind them, but pay attention to how the ball reacts and rolls. You can learn a lot about the pace of the green even if you are putting from a separate section of the green.

Make use of any clues around the green even if they come from your opponent.

Use playing order to your advantage

There are various aspects of the rules of playing order that you can use. If you are participating in a strokeplay match and you find yourself head-to-head with a gritty opponent, it is always best to hole out first, to add pressure to their putt. In strokeplay, you are allowed to play out of turn and hole a short putt if you wish. It is often best to get this out of the way and pressurize the opposition. In matchplay, you may be given many short putts, but if you play out of turn your opponent can ask you to replay the shot; there is no penalty for this.

Fourball tactics

When you are playing fourball, better-ball matches, you must use playing order to your advantage. If it is your side's turn to putt, is does not matter whose ball you play. You can take the shorter putt first to secure a par, for example, meaning the player with the birdie chance can putt aggressively without worrying about the return.

When playing fourballs, use the order of play to your advantage.

Technical tactics

There is a specific approach you can have towards your technique that will help iron out inconsistencies and problems. Here are some suggestions on how to overcome the most common problems on the green and a look at how the best putters size up their putts.

Keep your body still

Most putts are missed through too much lower body movement as the golfer looks up eagerly to see where the ball has finished. Try propping a club against your backside as you practise putting so that it is carefully balanced and resting on the ground.

As you putt, concentrate on keeping the club in place. If your lower body wobbles or moves, the club will drop to the ground. You have to remain steady to hold it in position, which will make your stroke more consistent.

Putting myth – 'put topspin on your putts'

This is a common piece of advice often dispensed by magazines and books. The theory behind the advice is sound enough but a more accurate expression would be 'make your putts roll end over end'. If you try to put topspin on your putts, you will hit the ball with the bottom of your putter. Look to hit the ball at the base of your stroke with the full face of the putter making contact with the centre of the ball. This leads to a consistent end-over-end roll.

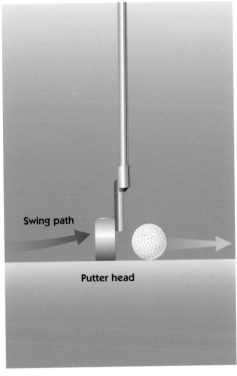

Swing path

Putter head

Keep a steady eye on the putt

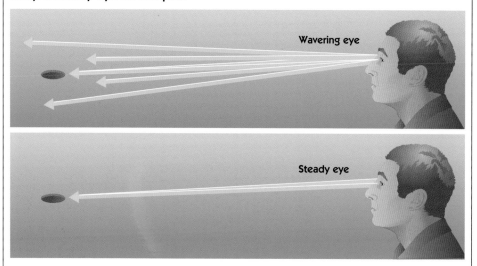

Research in North America has revealed a marked difference in the way a good and a bad putter physically look at the putt. After extensive research, scientists at the University of Calgary in Canada discovered that a good putter will maintain a steady look at specific points on the ball, the hole and the path of the putt. Poor putters' eyes swivel around the objects, never settling on any one specific point for a long time, leading to confusing messages to the brain and missed putts.

Keep your eye steady to hole more putts

• Concentrate on the hole: pick a specific point on the hole as a target, such as a mark or a blade of grass.

• Watch the ball drop: in your mind's eye, watch the ball roll over your point and drop.

• Shift your view smoothly: move your eye-line smoothly down the line of the putt from ball to hole to rest on the back of the ball.

• Stay steady: keep a still, focused and specific point on the ball in mind as you putt.

Comfort – the ultimate tactic

Putting well is all down to comfort. If you are happy and comfortable with your technique, then you will play to your ability. For this reason, don't be afraid to change and tweak your grip, stance or posture if you feel you have gone stale or have lost form on the greens.

MOVING FORWARD

Once you have mastered the basics, there is only one real way to improve constantly and that is through playing. You have to put the hours in on the course, on the practice putting green, learning from experience and mistakes. But one essential element is often overlooked when it comes to putting – a lesson.

Practise, practise, practise

You have to put those hours in on the putting green to see marked improvements. Use the drills, games and ideas in this book to make practice interesting and make sure you know you are doing the right thing. Practice does not make perfect; practice makes permanent.

Watch and learn from the very best

Golf gets under your skin and you can't leave it alone. You'll follow it endlessly through magazines or on television. You won't be able to get enough of it. Make use of your thirst for the game by taking notes on what you can see from the pros.

Why bother with a putting lesson?

The putter is the club in the bag you use most often – unless you are a master chipper – you use it on 90 per cent of holes. Putting is around 50 per cent of the game, yet it is probably the element that golfers practise least. If you go for a lesson, you want the pro to sort out your slice and forget about the constant three-putts. The quickest and simplest way to shave five shots a round is through better putting – better putting comes via lessons.

As with all golf lessons, though, success will not happen overnight. You need to practise and drill the advice you've been given. Often, you may find there is an initial dip in your form but taking one step back to make giant leaps forward is perfectly normal.

At a professional tournament

This is a great opportunity to see how golfers manage themselves around the course and the greens. Follow one or two pros for a number of holes. Learn from their pre-shot routine and how they read breaks. How often are they left with slippy downhill putts? How often do they three-putt and how do they react?

Women are better than men

If you are a mid- to high-handicap male golfer, watching a professional women's event is more constructive than watching the Open Championship or the Masters. Top women hit the ball the same distance and play the course in a similar way to many male amateurs, although much more consistently.

Watching golf on television

Take a note of how professionals judge pace. Their judgement of pace is very good and this comes from the gentle, unhurried touch they have with their strokes. Note where the ball regularly finishes when they miss – always beyond the hole and rarely short. How do they cope under pressure or when things go wrong?

Playing in a Pro-Am or going to a clinic

This is a great chance for hands-on advice but be wary of many players. Unless the pro has a coaching background, their advice is more likely to suit them as opposed to you. They are immensely talented and have a method that works for them but it may not be perfect for you. Do, though, take advice on shot selection and tactics.

Good and bad practice

It is fantastic if you have managed to spend a good stint on the practice putting greens, but you must be careful not to let your hard work actually do more damage than good. Bad practice can be destructive for your game.

Focus fully

Spending two hours on the green is no good if you have simply putted aimlessly. All you'll end up with is a bad back. Every session must have a goal and a route to reach that end. Whether your aim is to improve your alignment, touch or rhythm, a specific resolution is essential. Build into the relevant drills, exercises and games that will make your time productive.

Find your level

There is no point in spending hours on the green purely so that you can say you've been working hard at your game. Make sure you only spend the time on the green that you wish. Different golfers have different levels of endurance. Find yours and organize your sessions around this.

Stick to your routine

Practice is a rehearsal of intent. You want to replicate your consistency and skill on the practice green when you are on the course. As this is the case, you should, when you are on the practice green, replicate the way that you play for real, which means running through your pre-putt routine with every shot and taking each putt seriously. You will find your practice much more effective if you do this.

Variety is the spice of any putting session

To make your hours of putting practice most prosperous, find one or more practice partners and either work together on similar elements or create competition. A great way to keep each other inspired is to invent golf circuit training.

Practise with friends to help your motivation.

• With a friend, organize an hour-long session. Limiting the time will focus the mind and the exercises.

• Think of a variety of drills and practices you can do on different sections of the green.

• Vary between stamina (holing ten putts from a short distance in succession) technique and touch drills. It is essential to switch between drills that centre on the hole and putts that are less result-orientated.

• Build up a scoring system where you are able to compete in each discipline.

• You could even build a self-judging system where you mark the quality of each other's strokes.

• Expand the practice to take in chipping and even approach play, creating a golfing triathalon.

Use squad rotation

To keep putting practice interesting and to freshen your putting technique, alternate between different grips. Try left hand over right, or the claw grip, or use a different putter. This stimulates your mind because the brain gets bored with a repetitive task. Often, when someone gives you a new putter, you putt well with it – so keep changing in practice to keep your technique fresh – it doesn't matter if you use these new techniques on the course or not.

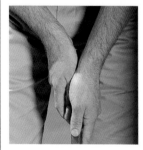

Keep trying out new grips even if you don't use them on the course.

Tips from the top

Here are six of the best putting tips from six of the best putters and coaches in the world – these are the right people to learn from when it comes to practical and instantly usable advice.

Tight grip for short putts

Fred Couples advocates using a slightly tighter grip for holing short putts. The theory is that this will help to keep the putter low to the ground as it strikes. Other pros use alternative techniques over short putts, including Champions Tour player Steve Stultz who uses a broomhandle putter for short putts and an orthodox putter for medium and longer shots.

Keep your left elbow pointed at the ball-to-target line.

Listen to the ball strike the clubface.

Keep that left elbow bent

Bobby Jones' key thought when putting was to point his left elbow at his ball-to-target line when at address. With such a technique, he was able to rock his shoulders more freely and had no need to worry about an over-active left hand.

Ignore technique – just listen

One of the greatest putters of all time, Ben Crenshaw, thinks that over-analysing technique is destructive. His solution to avoid complicated instruction is to listen to the strike of the ball on the putterface. He believes you can always hear and feel a solid strike. Keep your tempo even, back and through, listen to that strike and putt well.

Don't force yourself into a change of technique

Davis Love III, one of the seven most successful golfers in the USA over the last two decades, thinks that amateurs get into trouble when they make practice strokes in the wrong place. He says that whenever you are preparing for a putt you must make your practice strokes parallel to the ball-to-target line. Then you can move into the shot for real without having to worry about any alignment issues – the practice stroke is a proper rehearsal of intent.

Practise putting with only one ball

Seve Ballesteros and Lee Trevino are renowned for their imagination, touch and flair on and around the greens. One of the secrets of their success is a quirky practice routine. They only ever practise with one ball. This forces them to run through the shot seriously, completing a proper pre-putt routine and obtaining a decent read. Most importantly, though, they learn more from the putt, as they only focused on that one ball. This was a great tool in developing imagination as they could experiment and learn quickly even if they weren't hitting too many balls.

Place a club behind the ball

Clive Tucker, one of *Golf Monthly*'s top 25 coaches in the UK, has a simple practice to improve your ball's roll on the green. Place a shaft behind the ball at right angles to the target line, then hit putts. The shaft acts as a barrier, meaning you can only strike the top half of the ball, which is the best area to produce end-over-end roll, essential for a perfect putt.

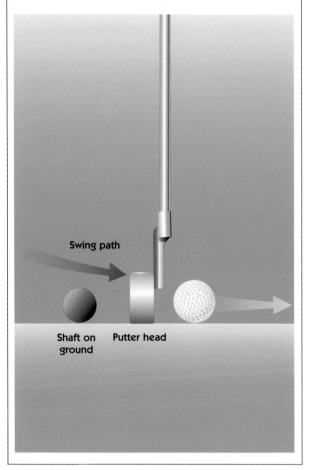

Swing path

Shaft on ground

Putter head

A–Z of Putting

Accelerating through the ball: when you are making a putt, the putterhead is moving more quickly – accelerating – when it makes contact with the ball than when you first took the putterhead back.

Apex of the putt: the point where the break of the green takes hold as the ball loses speed in the putt. It is the turning point of any particular putt.

Apron: the area of fairway at the front of the green, which is often sunk below the level of the putting surface.

Bare lie: when a ball rests on the ground with little or no grass beneath it, making it difficult to strike it cleanly.

Ball-to-target line: the direct line between your ball and the direction in which you want the ball to start rolling.

Belly putter: a type of putter with an extended shaft that rests in the belly at address.

Blocked or pushed putt: when a putt misses to the right of the hole because of a technical flaw in the stroke.

Borrow: an alternative word for 'break' on the putting green.

Broomhandle putter: a longer putter than the belly putter; when using the hands are split and the end of the shaft is held around the chest.

Dead weight: when the ball has rolled up next to the hole, stopping next to it – not beyond it or short – leaving a tiny putt to hole out.

Face-balanced putter: these putters have the weight evenly spread across the head. The head is usually large with a bulk of metal behind.

Fringe: the area of slightly longer grass that runs around the edge of the green.

Gimme: in matchplay, when a ball is so close to the hole that the putt is almost unmissable, the opposing golfer can concede the putt to save time. Giving or not giving putts can become strategic in matchplay.

Grain of the green: the direction the grass lies in is known as the grain. All grass will lie in one direction, usually pointing towards the sun.

Heel-toe putter: these have less metal behind the head and will balance more towards the shaft of the club.

Hold: another word for the grip – how your hands take 'hold' of the putter.

Inside the line to square: When the putterhead swings in a controlled arc on a line close to your body, as opposed to on a direct line from the ball.

Links course: a golf course that is built in the sand-dunes next to the sea, in the area that 'links' the sea with the land. This is where golf originated and is the most natural version of the sport, typically with fast greens.

Pace of the green: how far the ball rolls when it is putted. If the ball rolls far for a soft putt, this is a quick green, and vice versa.

Pitchmark: a hole on the green made by the ball when it lands. Depending on the softness and type of the green, any ball landing on the green from any distance is liable to make a mark and this needs repairing.

Poor strike: when the putterhead makes an off-centre connection with the ball, missing the sweet spot of the club and rolling poorly.

Pro-Am: a tournament, often played the day before a professional event, in which amateurs compete in teams with one professional, usually played as a Stableford format off full handicap.

Pulled putt: when a putt misses to the left of the hole, again as a result of faulty technique.

Pulling the trigger: the moment in the golf swing or putting stroke when you first take the club back before striking.

Putterface: the side of the club used to strike the ball.

Putterhead: the head of the club, incorporating the putterface.

Quick green: a green with very short grass on which the ball rolls fast for a soft stroke.

Release: hingeing of the wrists on the backstroke and rehingeing on the through stroke. In your full swing, your forearms will also rotate.

Roll: the manner in which the ball moves towards the hole once putted – you can have a 'good' or a 'bad' roll.

Straight back and through: when the putterhead swings in a direct line with the target as you make your stroke – it does not move from parallel.

Up-and-down: when a golfer holes out in two shots from off the green, usually when chipping. This often takes the form of a chip close to the hole followed by a short putt.

INDEX

Acknowledgements

The author and publisher would like to extend grateful thanks to **The London Golf Club** for their generosity and hospitality during the photoshoot. And also to Daniel Webb, Andy Smith, Craig Brown, Danielle Gibb and Jordan Gibb for taking part.

Executive Editor Trevor Davies
Project Editor Kate Tuckett
Executive Art Editor Leigh Jones
Designer Tony Truscott
Special Photography Steve Bardens
Artwork BrindeauMexter
Production Manager Ian Paton
Picture Researcher Sophie Delpech

Octopus Publishing Group Limited/Angus Murray 2, 8, 9, 14 left, 14 right, 16 bottom, 20 left, 20 right, 28 left, 28 right, 28 centre, 29 left, 29 right, 29 centre, 34 bottom, 46, 48, 50 left, 50 right, 50 centre, 53 top left, 53 bottom right, 55 top, 57, 58, 63, 65 Top, 65 bottom left, 69, 70, 80, 86, 88, 102 left, 102 right, 103 top left, 103 top right, 103 bottom right, 103 bottom left, 111, 113, 113 top, 119, 121 top, 121 centre right, 121 bottom right, 122 left, 122 right, 125; /Mark Newcombe 76 top.